EVEN TODAY, IN OUR WORLD, THERE ARE REIGNS SUPREME. THEY MOST SPECTACULAR EARTH – REMOTE ICY POLAR WASTES, GREAT TRACTS OF SOME REMARKABLE DEPEND ON THESE WILD

2 CASCADE MOUNTAINS

Some of the highest snowfalls in the world have been recorded in the Cascade Mountains, a range that runs parallel to North America's Pacific coast. Intercepting moisture-laden oceanic wind, the west-facing slopes of Mount Baker and the range's other highest peaks have recorded snowfalls of more than 25 m a year. Dense forests thrive in the damp conditions on these slopes, while farther inland the landscape becomes much drier. Many of the peaks in the Cascades are active volcanoes, including Mount St Helens, which erupted on May 18, 1980, sweeping away a huge area of forest and smothering the region downwind with ash. Six other volcanoes in the Cascades have erupted in the past 200 years.

Different species of pika live high up on rocky mountain slopes in northern Europe, Asia and North America, including in the Cascades. These small mammals are plant-eaters, and they also dry plants and store them as a kind of hay in their burrows to be used as winter food. Although pikas look like rodents, they are actually lagomorphs – related to rabbits and hares.

PIKA

1 GALAPAGOS ISLANDS

Over thousands of years, the remoteness of the Galápagos Islands, combined with their harsh terrain, has produced some remarkable animals that are found nowhere else on Earth. Lying on the Equator, nearly 1000 km west of South America, the Galápagos were desert islands until first seen by Europeans in the mid-16th century. Unique species include the Galápagos giant tortoise, which feeds on cacti and other plants, and weighs up to 300 kg, and the Galápagos penguin, the only penguin that lives on the Equator. Another endemic species is the world's only marine iguana (right). The marine iguana's ability to feed in the sea, diving beneath the waves to graze on seaweed, makes it unique among lizards. Between dives, the iguanas spread out on rocks to reheat their bodies in the Sun.

3 P

Fed
is South A
of Brazil, B
annual floo
Pantanal sw
Britain. Its
of the riche
species incl
alligators a
world's larg
also home t
thousand
the h
pa

WILD PLACES

The range and diversity of the world's wild places embrace snowy mountain peaks, lush green rain forests and eerie deserts. Each place is unique, shaped by a particular combination of climate, location and landscape. In some, such as the Galápagos Islands, isolation has allowed species to evolve that are unknown elsewhere. In others, such as the Florida Everglades, most species exist elsewhere but are rarely found together in such variety or abundance. Earth's wild places reveal the sheer majesty, inventiveness and resilience of nature.

Alligator holes are a key part of life in the Everglades. Alligators dig these water-filled depressions in the ground with their snouts and claws to use as refuges during the dry winter months. Their holes also provide important habitats for the birds and fish of the Everglades, which live safely alongside a hole's owner because alligators stop feeding when they are cold.

FASCINATING FACT

4 EVERGLADES

The largest subtropical wetland the United States lies across the southern tip of Florida. Instead of open water, the Everglades consists mainly of a huge expanse of sharp-edged sawgrass, interspersed with channels and pools. Famous for birds – such as the great white egret (left) – and alligators, the Everglades also teems with turtles, snakes and nearly 100 species of fish. Mammals include a rare subspecies of panther, the Florida panther, and the manatee, a huge aquatic mammal that lives in shallow water, feeding on algae and mangrove leaves.

ANTANAL

by the Paraguay River, the Pantanal
erica's largest wetland, covering parts
livia and Paraguay. During the river's
, when it rises by up to 5 m, the
ells to cover an area the size of
mmense mosaic of waterways is one
t wildlife habitats in the world, whose
de the spectacled caiman, related to
d crocodiles, and the capybara, the
est rodent (right). The Pantanal is
cougars, giant otters and nearly a
species of birds, including toucans,
acinth macaw (the world's largest
rot, up to 1 m long) and the huge
jabiru stork, up to 1.5 m tall.

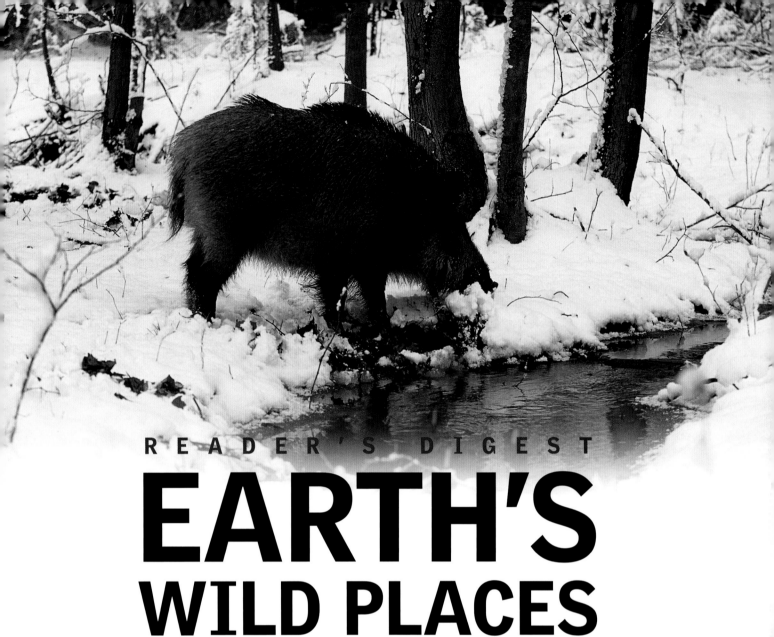

READER'S DIGEST

EARTH'S
WILD PLACES

1 SUPREME ISOLATION

2 DESERT WILDERNESS

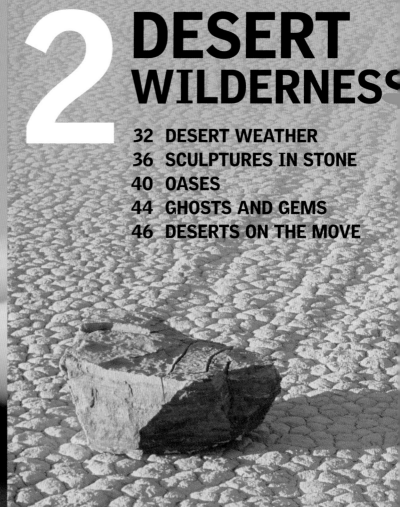

5 PRIMEVAL FORESTS

6 LOST HORIZONS

3 INSULATED BY COLD

4 HIGHS AND LOWS

7 FRESHWATER WILDERNESS

8 WILD COASTS

INTRODUCTION

DEEP IN PREHISTORY, OUR DISTANT ANCESTORS LIVED IN A WORLD THAT WAS WHOLLY WILD. There were no tracks, no fences, no permanent dwellings of any kind. The modern world could hardly be more different: we live on a planet dominated by people, where half the global population lives in huge cities and towns. Yet even in today's crowded world, wild places survive. From far-flung mountain peaks rising like islands in the sky to vast regions of desert and wilderness, these wild environments often provide a last refuge for plant and animal species under pressure from human activity.

In some places, sheer **isolation** ensures the survival of a wilderness, nowhere more so than in Earth's remotest location – **Bouvet Island** in the Southern Ocean, separated from its nearest land neighbour by hundreds of miles of storm-tossed sea. Off the north-western coast of Scotland, the remote island group of **St Kilda** is one of Europe's most haunting wild places, home to breeding seabirds, seals and turtles. Compared to these scraps of land, the **polar regions** cover huge areas, but a similar isolation from the human world prevails. Nearly 40 000 people visit **Antarctica** on ships each year, but when the polar summer ends, the tourists vanish, the sea freezes over and the long winter night begins. During the coldest

months, the only human presence is a skeleton staff of scientists, yet this hostile habitat is home to thousands of penguins, who flock there to breed.

Some wild places are reminders of a time when most of the planet was in nature's hands. Africa's **Okavango Delta** and Florida's **Everglades** are the result of geological flukes, which have created fantastically rich habitats for **wildlife**. In other places, the climate is so harsh that people have always been thin on the ground. The largest of these wildernesses are **deserts**, such as Chile's **Atacama**, and other wide-open tracts, including Australia's treeless **Nullarbor Plain**, one and a half times the size of England, where only the hardiest animals, such as kangaroos and camels, thrive. At the other extreme are ancient or 'old growth' **forests**, with no far horizons, just a seamless panorama of trees. The greatest of these wooded wildernesses is the boreal forest or **taiga**, which stretches across northern Europe, Asia and North America. In eastern Europe, the **Bialowieza Forest** is a surviving portion of the wildwood that once covered most of the continent. Other ancient fragments include the rain forests of western **Tasmania** and the wind-blasted southern beeches that endure the lashing of storms near **Cape Horn** – all bearing witness to nature's untamed power, still able to inspire awe and wonder in our high-tech world.

SUPREME ISOLATION

1

REMOTE ST KILDA (LEFT), ON THE WESTERNMOST FRINGES OF SCOTLAND'S OUTER HEBRIDES, WAS ONCE HOME TO A CLOSE-KNIT ISLAND COMMUNITY. The last islanders were evacuated in 1930 after a succession of failed harvests, ending 2000 years of human habitation on this isolated Atlantic outpost. Today, St Kilda's only human residents are conservation staff and military personnel, but it is home to thousands of seabirds. Cut off from the outside world by their location, or by hazardous coasts that make it difficult to land, oceanic islands like St Kilda include the remotest pieces of land on Earth. Many provide precious breeding grounds for seabirds, turtles and seals, and some offer a last safe haven for animals, such as New Zealand's kakapo parrot and Australia's quokka, that are endangered or extinct on the nearby mainland.

ISLANDS FAR FROM ANYWHERE

THE WORLD'S MOST ISOLATED SPECKS OF LAND RISE FROM THE IMMENSE SWEEP OF THE SOUTHERN OCEAN. They include the remotest island on Earth – Bouvet Island, a mass of ice-covered rock, which lies more than 1600 km from the coast of Antarctica, the nearest land. Bouvet's appearance on the map dates from the 1730s, when a French explorer, Jean-Baptiste Bouvet, set sail from Brittany on a journey to the edge of the world. At the time, most scientists believed that the Southern Hemisphere contained unexplored landmasses, which counterbalanced the land in the north. Bouvet's task was to find them, chart them and claim them in the name of France. It seemed simple enough, but the reality was quite the reverse.

What Bouvet found was the vast emptiness of the Southern Ocean. Instead of coastlines broken with occasional natural harbours, there was just open ocean, in which his ships – the *Aigle* and the *Marie* – had to cope with mountainous waves. As the expedition kept to its southerly course, it left behind all known sea routes, and despite the long days of the far southern summer the horizon remained obstinately blank for week after week. Then, on New Year's Day 1739, a shout came from the *Aigle*. The lookout had spotted land.

The discovery almost defies belief. Quite by chance, Bouvet and his shipmates had stumbled across the world's most isolated piece of land, which now bears Bouvet's name. Just 11 km across, Bouvet Island is shaped like a blunt-ended egg lying on its side. Ice covers more than nine-tenths of it, masking the outline of an extinct volcano, which rose from the seabed millions of years ago. The only bare land consists of black lava shelves close to the shore – the world's most far-flung breeding site for seals and seabirds.

Volcanic islands rarely have natural harbours, and Bouvet is no exception. Unable to find a landing point, Jean-Baptiste Bouvet eventually gave up and sailed away. The island was not seen again for more than 80 years, partly because the explorer had made an error in his log, placing it several dozen nautical miles to the east of its true position. This was finally established in 1808 by the captain of a British whaling ship.

A breeding haven

Bouvet Island has never been inhabited and probably never will be, but other islands in the far south have had a human presence, despite their unwelcoming climate. One is Macquarie Island – a grass-covered rib of volcanic rock just under 35 km long. It lies on a submarine ridge that reaches north from Antarctica to Australia. Unlike Bouvet Island, Macquarie is too far north for permanent ice, and the rocky beaches on its eastern flank are sheltered from the wind. In spring and summer, these teem with penguins and seals, sparring noisily in the annual race to breed. Humans arrived in the 19th century, when Macquarie Island became an outpost for seal-hunters (see page 23).

EDGE OF ANTARCTICA An iceberg drifts off the coast of Elephant Island, named for its elephant seals. In 1916 Ernest Shackleton's crew spent four months on the island, waiting for the rescue that arrived on August 30.

They brought rabbits, cats and rats, which soon gained a foothold in the wild. Although cats have since been eradicated, rabbits and rats continue to threaten the island's penguin colonies.

Escape from Elephant Island

Closer to Antarctica, a string of islands, including the South Orkneys and South Shetlands, stretches north and east along the edge of the Weddell Sea. In April 1916 they were the backdrop for Antarctica's greatest human survival story – the rescue of the

Shackleton expedition. More than two dozen men, under the command of Ernest Shackleton, had planned to cross Antarctica on foot, but their ship, *Endurance*, was destroyed by winter ice. Shackleton ordered the men into the ship's lifeboats and steered northwards to Elephant Island, off the tip of the Antarctic Peninsula. Then, taking four men with him, he set off for the island of South Georgia, nearly 1300 km away, which had a whaling station. The journey took 14 days, but he made it to raise the alarm and get help. In the end, all 22 men left behind were rescued.

LONELY OUTPOST The white breasts of royal penguins stand out against the dark volcanic sand on Macquarie Island. Adult penguins return to the same spot each year to breed.

COMPARED WITH MOST OFFSHORE ISLANDS – INCLUDING THOSE THAT MAKE UP BRITAIN AND IRELAND – volcanic islands, such as Hawaii, Madeira and Tristan da Cunha, are newcomers in the oceans. Offshore islands are fragments of continent that have been cut off by the sea – they have the same rocks as the nearby continental mainland, laid down in layers over hundreds of millions of years. Volcanic islands, in contrast, sit above faults, or hotspots, in the seabed and their growth can be phenomenal as they blast their way upwards to the surface. Found in the farthest reaches of the oceans, they include some of the most isolated places on Earth.

Lava and ash, eroded over time by the sea and rain, are the raw materials that make up these islands. Lava is hard, which makes it good at resisting erosion, but volcanic ash is often as crumbly as a cake. Rain gouges

OVER THE VOLCANO

out deep ravines and sweeps the ash downhill onto beaches of dark volcanic sand. With so much blackness all around, volcanic islands might be sombre places, and in cold climates they often are. But where the climate is mild and damp, they are frequently brilliant green because volcanic ash is a natural fertiliser, packed with the minerals that plants need in order to grow. In the Hawaiian Islands, some plants have leaves as big as parasols, while in the Canaries fleshy-leaved succulents look like cabbages sprouting from the rocks. Madeira is famous for its wines and its glorious displays of wild flowers. Together, these far-flung islands make up a botanist's paradise with numerous plant species found nowhere else in the world.

Sleeping giants

On some of the islands, volcanic activity has faded away, but on many it is still very much alive. With volcanoes, big does not always mean dangerous, and this is particularly true when they emerge from the deep seabed. One of the world's greatest volcanoes, Kilauea on the island of Hawaii, erupts almost continuously, producing rivers of molten lava that make the water boil where they flow into the sea. Yet

Where the climate is mild and damp, volcanic islands are frequently brilliant green because volcanic ash is a natural fertiliser, packed with the minerals that plants need in order to grow.

despite being so large and active, Kilauea poses little threat to life on Hawaii. Because the lava is thin and runny, it quickly flows away, which means that the volcano simmers gently, instead of building up pressure and exploding in cataclysmic bursts.

Kilauea is distinctive in another way, too. While most volcanoes are found along the edges of the tectonic plates that make up the Earth's crust, Kilauea sits over an isolated point of volcanic heat, called a hotspot. The Hawaiian hotspot has remained in place for millions of years, while the seabed above it has been pushed north-westwards by continental drift. The result is a string of islands, which formed over the hotspot on the seabed and then drifted on. They range from Hawaii itself, almost directly above the hotspot today, to Kure Atoll, more than 2000 km away. The smallest islands in the chain are among the oldest and are only rarely visited, leaving nature firmly in control. The most conspicuous residents are seabirds and brightly coloured hermit crabs, which pick their way over the coral-fringed shore.

Fire and ice

In the Atlantic Ocean, volcanic energy has created the world's most widely spaced island chain. Altogether, this contains less than two

dozen islands, spread out from the Arctic Circle to the Antarctic, a total distance of nearly 10 000 km. The thread that unites them is the Mid-Atlantic Ridge, an undersea mountain chain, which runs roughly down the middle of the Atlantic. It marks the zone where two tectonic plates are slowly separating, allowing magma to emerge and new seabed to form. The central part of the ridge is highly volcanic, and this is where the islands rise.

The northernmost of the mid-Atlantic islands is Jan Mayen, a bleak ice-covered fleck of land between Greenland and Norway, well inside the Arctic Circle. It is dominated by the world's most northerly active volcano, which last erupted in 1985. Despite the bleak scenery, with jet black rock often covered by a blanket of snow, Jan Mayen is not entirely lifeless. Arctic foxes manage to survive there, and in the brief Arctic summer the desolate coast throngs with seabirds.

From Jan Mayen, the Mid-Atlantic Ridge runs south-westwards until it reaches Iceland, where it emerges once more above sea level to create by far the biggest island in the chain.

BULLSEYE A satellite image (left) shows Queen Mary's Peak rising in the centre of Tristan da Cunha, a volcanic island that rises to the surface in water 4000 m deep.

ON THE EDGE Plumes of steam rise from volcanic vents on Tristan da Cunha, a sign that the island's volcano is still active.

Iceland has Europe's largest glacier, Vatnajökull, with several volcanoes hidden beneath its ice, their heat creating extensive lakes as they melt the ice. In 1996 one of the volcanoes erupted and an enormous torrent of meltwater surged towards the sea. Volcanologists had picked up early warning signs of the eruption and despite the incredible scale of the flood, no one was hurt.

Although bigger than Ireland, Iceland has a population of just 300 000, two-thirds of whom live in or near the capital, Reykjavik. Most of the island is a wilderness of geysers, spectacular waterfalls and black volcanic cliffs. For wildlife, one of the most important habitats is Lake Myvatn in the north of the island, a magnet for breeding water birds, formed by a volcanic eruption more than 2000 years ago.

Just south of Iceland, the ridge reaches the island of Surtsey, which burst through the sea's surface as recently as 1963. For close on half a century, Surtsey has fought a constant battle with erosion by the waves, and its surface area has shrunk by nearly half since 1963. Despite this, the island is home to many kinds of seabird and more than 50 plant species. Most of the plants arrived on the island carried by the wind, although birds and driftwood have also inadvertently transported seeds.

South of Surtsey, the Mid-Atlantic Ridge remains beneath the waves for nearly 2400 km until it comes to the Azores, the next stop in the island chain. With a mild and damp climate, the Azores have been settled since the 15th century and are now an autonomous region of Portugal, but their green forests and pastures hide a violent past. Some of their volcanic craters are more than 2 km across – evidence of colossal eruptions in the days before human inhabitants arrived.

On the rocks

From the Azores, the ridge curves south and east towards the Equator. Just before crossing this, it rises to the surface once again, but this time there are no craters or towering volcanoes – just a scattering of rocks that are all less than 20 m high. The St Peter and St Paul Rocks lie 1000 km east of Brazil, and they have no freshwater, almost no vegetation and no human inhabitants. On this tiny archipelago, there is little sign of life apart from terns and other seabirds.

The St Peter and St Paul Rocks are geologically unique and have long fascinated scientists – Charles Darwin visited them in 1832 during his round-the-world voyage on the *Beagle*.

GREEN GEM Madeira is a lush volcanic island rising from the African tectonic plate to the east of the Mid-Atlantic Ridge. The Portuguese started to settle the island around 1420.

EXIT ROUTE Small 'parasitic' craters dot the barren slopes of Ascension Island. They form when the main crater becomes blocked and lava finds another route to the surface.

Unlike other mid-Atlantic islands, they are not the result of volcanic eruptions. Instead, the ridge is simply so high here that it breaks the surface – the only place in the world where a mid-ocean ridge does this.

Turtle breeding grounds

From the St Peter and St Paul Rocks, the Mid-Atlantic Ridge heads almost due south towards its end in the Southern Ocean. The next land is Ascension Island – so called because a Portuguese navigator, Afonso de Albuquerque, sighted it on Ascension Day 1503. Ascension Island lies inside the tropics. Its highest mountain is pockmarked with dozens of craters, and much of the island consists of dry and desolate lava flows. None of this matters for seabirds and green turtles because the island has one vital commodity – land where they can breed.

Boobies, terns and tropicbirds all nest on the island, as do green turtles. Every year, up to 5000 female turtles fight their way through the pounding surf to haul themselves onto the black sand, where they dig nests and lay their eggs. Green turtles live in tropical waters all around the world, but the ones that breed on Ascension Island all come from the east coast of Brazil, about 2000 km away to the west. Since Ascension Island is just 12 km across, their journey is one of the most remarkable feats of navigation in the animal world.

Biologists are still unsure exactly how Ascension Island's turtles find their way to their volcanic island breeding ground. The most likely explanation is that they use a combination of clues, including the sea's smell and the Earth's magnetic field. Explaining why they do it is even more difficult. Their behaviour

may date back to the time when the island was still young. A single female turtle may have drifted off course and discovered the island's virgin beaches. Once these eggs had been laid, the species' strong homing instinct made sure that breeding turtles would return.

Islanders return

After Ascension Island, the Mid-Atlantic Ridge heads out of the tropics and does not break the surface until Tristan da Cunha, 3000 km away. Named after a Portuguese sailor who discovered it in 1506, Tristan da Cunha is part of an archipelago consisting of five islands and islets. One of them, Inaccessible Island, is the home of the world's smallest flightless bird, the Inaccessible Island rail. A distant relative of moorhens and coots, it is not much longer than a house sparrow, although it has strong legs and long toes – vital equipment for life in its windswept home.

Tristan da Cunha is the world's remotest inhabited island, with a population of about 250 people. The islanders do not often make the world's headlines, but in 1961 Tristan da Cunha's volcano, Queen Mary's Peak, began to erupt from a vent near the chief town. It was the first eruption in the island's recorded history, and it caused alarm both on the island and in the UK, which administers the territory. The entire population was evacuated to the UK, giving many of them their first trip abroad. The eruption was short-lived, and having seen the outside world almost all of the islanders chose to return home.

Beyond Tristan da Cunha, the Mid-Atlantic Ridge finally makes landfall at Bouvet Island (see page 16). Located midway between Africa and Antarctica, Bouvet is often hidden in the folds in maps – a fitting tribute to the remotest place of all.

RELICS OF THE PAST

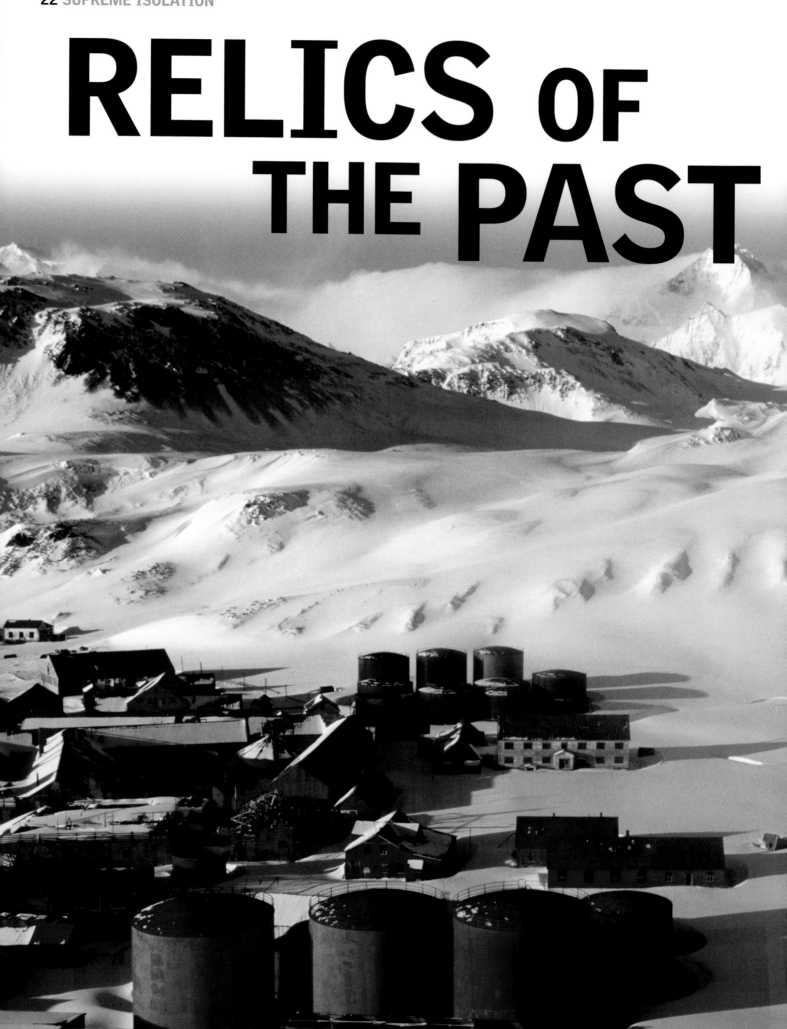

RUSTING CAST-IRON TANKS, RUINED BUILDINGS AND OTHER SIGNS OF HUMAN HABITATION SURVIVE on South Georgia and a few other islands of the Southern Ocean. Today, most visitors to these islands are tourists on cruise liners bound for Antarctica, but the debris points to a rather different past, when seals, whales and even penguins were caught for their meat, fat and oil.

Seal-hunters first arrived in the Southern Ocean in the late 18th century, drawn by reports of the huge numbers of fur seals that came ashore on sub-Antarctic beaches. The sealers' hunting methods were crude, but they could be devastatingly effective. Once a breeding colony was located, the carnage was indiscriminate, with youngsters and females killed for their fur, and males targeted for their leather. Whatever their age or sex, all seals provided blubber – a greasy fat that was boiled down, or 'rendered', in iron tanks, known as trypots, and turned into oil. Seal oil smelled rank, but it had lots of uses, from a fuel for lanterns to an ingredient in soap.

The sealers made good profits, but their impact in the Southern Ocean was catastrophic. When the South Shetland Islands were discovered in 1819, more than a quarter of a million fur seals crowded along their coastline. Just three years later, after the sealers had done their work, the South Shetland seals

RECLAIMED BY NATURE Fur seal pups play among cast-iron pots that were once used to boil down members of their kind to extract oil.

had almost completely disappeared. The same story was repeated throughout the Southern Ocean as sealers hunted far and wide. By the 1850s, seal stocks were so low that the sealing trade itself had almost become extinct.

Whaling stations

Processing seals was relatively straightforward, because they were caught and butchered on land. The Southern Ocean had another, much bigger source of oil and meat that required more complicated processing – the world's largest whales. In 1902, Carl Anton Larsen, a Norwegian, made an exploratory trip south and was amazed by the number of whales he saw in the waters around South Georgia. He decided to take a financial gamble and set up Grytviken, the world's southernmost whaling station.

The decision proved profitable. In its first year alone, the Grytviken station processed 183 whales, and in the second the number rose to 399. Many were blue whales – huge animals up to 30 m long that could weigh more than 100 tonnes. After being towed to Grytviken, the whales were winched up a slipway, then cut up into pieces, or 'flensed'. The fat was boiled down, while the meat was salted to preserve it.

A supply ship visited each spring, but apart from that Grytviken was entirely self-sufficient. It had its own power station, hospital, cinema and a farm that raised chickens and pigs. A prefabricated church, brought from Norway, was consecrated on Christmas Day 1913 – the height of the southern summer.

Other companies soon established whaling stations on islands throughout the Southern Ocean, until the 1920s when land-based stations started to be superseded by floating factory ships. As the catch continued to rise almost exponentially, the whale population crashed. In 1986, the International Whaling Commission finally acted to stop the slaughter of the Southern Ocean's whales, allowing these magnificent creatures to begin the long slow journey to recovery.

STANDING APART Grytviken was a bustling town when its church was built in 1913. The church is still a functioning place of worship, serving South Georgia's shifting summertime population, which includes research scientists and cruise-ship tourists.

ISLAND SANCTUARIES

EVERY SUMMER, CITY-DWELLERS TAKE A SHORT FERRY RIDE FROM PERTH IN WESTERN AUSTRALIA TO ROTTNEST ISLAND JUST OFFSHORE. With its cool ocean breezes, Rottnest is a good place to escape the heat.

It is also the last stronghold of the quokka – one of many animals that depend on islands for their survival. Rottnest literally means 'rat's nest', a name given to it by Dutch explorers, who had never seen marsupials before. Sailing along the Australian coast in the late 17th century, they often caught quokkas for food.

At the time quokkas, along with many other marsupials, were also common on the Australian mainland, but as European settlers arrived that soon changed. With Europeans came foxes, cats and rabbits – animals that either prey on quokkas or compete

SAFETY IN NUMBERS Rottnest Island's population of about 10 000 quokkas is large enough to assure the species' future.

with them for food. Faced with these alien invaders, most of Australia's small and medium-sized marsupials found themselves on the retreat. Some – like the pig-footed bandicoot – eventually became extinct, but the quokka had a crucial fallback position. Its range included a number of offshore islands that European mammals never managed to reach. The largest of these was Rottnest, where quokkas still live today.

Island of the mammoths

Throughout history, offshore islands have been places where species on the retreat have made their last stand. One of the most remarkable examples is Wrangel Island, a desolate slab of tundra, more than 100 km across, separated by the icy waters of the Arctic Ocean from the marshy mainland of eastern Siberia.

During the last ice age, woolly mammoths were widespread throughout the Arctic and sub-Arctic, but after the climate started to warm up around 12 000 years ago, most of

them became extinct. An exception to this trend was a pygmy form, standing just 1.8 m high at the shoulder and weighing up to 2 tonnes, which managed to survive until much more recent times on Wrangel Island. The reduced size of these miniature mammoths matched the small food supply on their island home. According to radiocarbon dating, they may finally have died out between 4000 and 3700 years ago.

Forced moves

No one helped quokkas or mammoths to reach their island sanctuaries – they either became cut off by rising sea levels or made the journey themselves. For some of today's rarest animals, being deliberately exiled is a last resort in the conservation battle to save them from extinction. This is what has happened to the kakapo, the world's heaviest parrot and the only one among more than 300 parrot species that cannot fly.

Kakapos are native to New Zealand, one of the last major landmasses to be discovered and settled by humans. The first human arrivals were Polynesians, who began to colonise the islands about 1200 years ago. They encountered an extraordinary world, which had no mammals apart from bats, but abounded in flightless birds. The largest of them were the moas, which stood up to 3.6 m high. Moas had few defences against human hunters and by the late 16th century all of them – numbering more than a dozen species – had gone. The kakapo

LATE DEVELOPER Kakapos are among the world's slowest breeding birds. Females take several years to reach sexual maturity, and if food is scarce they do not breed at all.

had the good fortune to be nocturnal, which made it harder to hunt. Even so, introduced mammals, including rats and stoats, decimated its eggs and young. Numbers plunged, and by the mid-1980s there were fewer than 60 kakapos left.

At this point, the Kakapo Recovery Plan was launched, which involved catching all the survivors and transferring them to four mammal-free islands scattered around New Zealand's coast. It seems that their enforced exile has paid off. Today, the total number of birds has climbed back into the 80s. Their island refuges hint at what New Zealand would have looked like before humans first stepped ashore – wild, rugged and breathtakingly beautiful, with some of the oddest wildlife on Earth.

PARROT REFUGE Codfish Island lies off Stewart Island, which lies off the southern end of New Zealand's South Island. It is home to about 30 kakapos, a third of the surviving population.

FLEETING GLIMPSES

SOME REMOTE ISLANDS ARE PARTICULARLY HARD TO PINPOINT SINCE THEY CAN DISAPPEAR – AND THEN SOMETIMES REAPPEAR. Sandbanks and cays are flat, intriguing and deceptively dangerous. Both structures are formed from sand which, like snow, comes in a multitude of different textures and colours – from the sand in sandbanks, often tinged grey by particles of silt, to the pure dazzling white of the coral sand that forms cays. Some sandbanks (see page 29) break the sea's surface as temporary islands when the tide is low, but then disappear again as the tide rises. Slivers of terra firma that build up on the highest points of coral reefs, cays are kept in place by currents, but they can vanish beneath the waves if a storm blows up and shifts their sand.

Cays (also spelt 'keys') are about as low as islands can get while still being classified as dry land. Some of the largest have been developed for

SLIPPING AWAY The narrow strip of coral sand called Whale-Skate Island is slowly shrinking as it fights a losing battle with erosion by the sea. It is one of the French Frigate Shoals in the Hawaiian island chain.

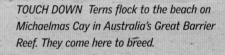

TOUCH DOWN *Terns flock to the beach on Michaelmas Cay in Australia's Great Barrier Reef. They come here to breed.*

tourism, but in the Caribbean Sea and the Indian and Pacific oceans many remain genuinely wild. Coral sand is very porous, so freshwater is hard to find, making the islands difficult for human habitation. These cays remain true island paradises, inhabited by wild animals, especially during the breeding season, when the air above them is filled with terns, noddies and tropicbirds shuttling between their nests and the open sea.

Off Australia's north-eastern coast, cays lie scattered along the whole length of the Great Barrier Reef, and there are more in the Coral Sea beyond the reef to the east. These remoter islets include the Lihou Cays, 18 islands arranged in a gigantic elongated ring, about 600 km east of the city of Cairns, on the very edge of Australia's continental shelf. One solitary cay lies still farther out: Heralds-Beacon Islet, perched on the Mellish Reef, an isolated coral platform about 1000 km from the Australian coast. At high tide, Heralds-Beacon Islet is only about 500 m wide and 100 m long, making it the ultimate 'desert island' – not necessarily dry, but absolutely deserted.

Every name has a story

Cays have always been given local names, but many of the names used today date from the time when European navigators started to chart tropical coasts. One of the first regions to be explored was the Caribbean. Here, European ships, on both official and unofficial (piratical or semi-piratical) business, nudged their way around cays from Florida southwards to Belize, where they encountered the world's second biggest barrier reef – one that forms along the coast of a continent or island, separated from it by a deep lagoon.

Occasionally, ships would become stuck fast on the coral, where there was a strong chance that their wooden hulls would get ripped apart – names like Cayo Muerto ('Dead Cay'), for an island off northern Nicaragua, show what could happen when things went badly wrong. The Dry Tortugas, at the end of the Florida Keys, show how important it was for vessels plying the tropical seas to find local sources of water and food. The islands lacked water but their turtles (*tortugas* in Spanish) provided

AMBERGRIS CAY OFF BELIZE OWES ITS NAME TO A DARK

grey waxy substance produced by sperm whales in their intestines. When a whale dies, hard lumps of its ambergris sometimes wash ashore – and did so in large quantities on the beaches of Ambergris Cay. In the past, ambergris was used in perfumes and fetched a high price.

ONE OF THE LARGEST UNDERWATER BANKS

in the world lies in the Indian Ocean north of Madagascar. The Saya de Malha Bank encompasses an area of 40 000 km².

THE HIGHEST POINT IN THE MALDIVE ISLANDS

is just 2 m above sea level.

food. Salt Cay in the Turks and Caicos Islands was known for its salinas (salt-drying pans), where salt, an important food preservative, was extracted from seawater.

In the Caribbean, most cays are clustered in groups, but there, too, lonely outposts of coral sand have formed above isolated reefs. Roncador Cay lies more than 400 km from the Nicaraguan coast with nothing but open sea due east until the Windward Islands, more than 1500 km away on the Caribbean's eastern rim. Although remote, Roncador has proved a hazard to shipping. In 1894 a US Navy sloop, the USS *Kearsage*, struck the reef and remains there to this day.

Coral sand is easily shifted by the waves, and several former islands off the tip of Florida have disappeared beneath the sea's surface, including Southwest Key, one of the Dry Tortugas, which sank out of sight in the 1870s. Another, Bird or Booby Key, disappeared in 1935. The remains of these islands now come perilously close to the surface at low tide, posing a danger to ships. Although bare cays are most at risk, even ones with a scattering of vegetation can be swept away by violent storms.

Atolls – volcanic remnants

In the northern Pacific, the French Frigate Shoals, part of the Hawaiian chain, are an example of an atoll – a cay or group of cays that forms over a ring-shaped reef. The islands are named after a French expedition that crossed the Pacific in 1786. The expedition's two ships had been sailing in open water when a lookout spotted breakers in their path. There was just enough time to alter course, avoiding disaster. This lucky escape proved to be only a temporary reprieve. In 1787 the ships set sail from the western Pacific for France, but were never seen again.

Atolls come in a number of shapes and sizes, from almost perfect circles to loops, as if a giant coil of rope had been thrown into the sea. The outer reef and beaches of an atoll are pounded by surf, which often makes an audible roar from several kilometres away. Together, they work like a security barrier, protecting the much calmer waters of a central lagoon. Here and there, the reef and its cays are intersected by deep channels, which connect the lagoon with the sea. When the tide is at full spate, the channels are like fast-running rivers, pouring either into the lagoon or out of it. The word 'atoll' originated in the Maldive Islands in the Indian Ocean, which consist entirely of atolls.

It was Charles Darwin, a biologist, who worked out how atolls form. The process begins when a large sea volcano erupts, and a new tropical island emerges above the waves. A coral reef develops on the volcano's underwater slopes, eventually encircling the island – a phase that can be seen in action around many tropical islands today. The next stage occurs when the volcano becomes extinct. The island starts to subside, but the reef keeps pace in the opposite direction: as the island erodes into the sea, the coral grows upwards towards the light. Finally, the volcano disappears beneath the waves, leaving behind the reef with its sandy cays poking above the surface.

> **The outer reef and beaches of an atoll are pounded by the surf. Together, they work like a security barrier, protecting the much calmer waters of a central lagoon.**

PEACE AND QUIET The Hawaiian monk seal, one of the world's rarest sea mammals, breeds on the coral beaches of the French Frigate Shoals. This mother is nursing a newborn pup.

The world's largest atoll is Great Chagos Bank, about 1600 km south-west of the tip of India. At its widest, its lagoon is more than 150 km across – so big that it is impossible to see across it, except from high up in the air. Yet despite the size of the atoll, the outer reef has only a scattering of cays, with a total land area of less than 5 km². One is Danger Island, probably so named because there were no safe places to anchor along its shores. Covered in palm trees, Danger Island has never had a permanent human presence, but in a good year it is home to more than 10 000 brown noddies, which lay their eggs there. Once the young can fly, they disappear out to sea, not returning to land for at least their first three years.

Ocean stepping stones

In the Pacific, early Polynesian navigators used atolls like stepping stones as they spread out across the ocean, making journeys that today seem breathtakingly daring. Over the course of many centuries, they managed to discover all of the Pacific's main island groups, as well as places like Easter Island, 3600 km of the coast of Chile, which are many days' travel from their nearest neighbour. According to one piece of evidence – the remains of an ancient chicken bone – these early seafarers may even have found their way to South America a hundred years before the arrival of Europeans.

BANKS OF SAND

UNLIKE CAYS, SANDBANKS ARE NOT CONFINED TO PLACES WHERE THE SEA IS WARM ENOUGH FOR CORAL TO GROW. Some sandbanks are colossal. In the English Channel, the Goodwin Sands off Kent are a huge mountain of sand, 19 km long and 8 km across at the widest point. When the tide is in, the bank lies hidden beneath the waves, but at low tide about a tenth of its area may be exposed, rising up to 4 m above sea level. Over the centuries, thousands of lives have been lost in shipwrecks on the Goodwin Sands, especially on the falling tide. Once a ship has run aground, currents can dig away the sand beneath it, until the vessel breaks its back.

According to local tradition, the Goodwin Sands once formed a low-lying island, called Lomea, where sheep grazed on fertile pasture until the sea swamped the farmland about a thousand years ago. Whatever the truth of this tradition, sandbanks are always changing and whole landscapes can be transformed in the process. That is what happened with Dogger Bank, an even bigger mass of sand and sediment, lying in the North Sea between England and Denmark. Today, the highest point in the Dogger Bank lies about 10 m beneath the sea's surface, but fossils show that the sandbank was once the home of large land animals. Lions, deer and mammoths all lived in 'Doggerland' during the last ice age, when sea levels were unusually low. As the climate warmed and the glaciers melted, Doggerland started to shrink. Finally, only the peaks of the great sandbank were visible, until they too disappeared beneath the waves even at low tide.

DESERT
WILDERN

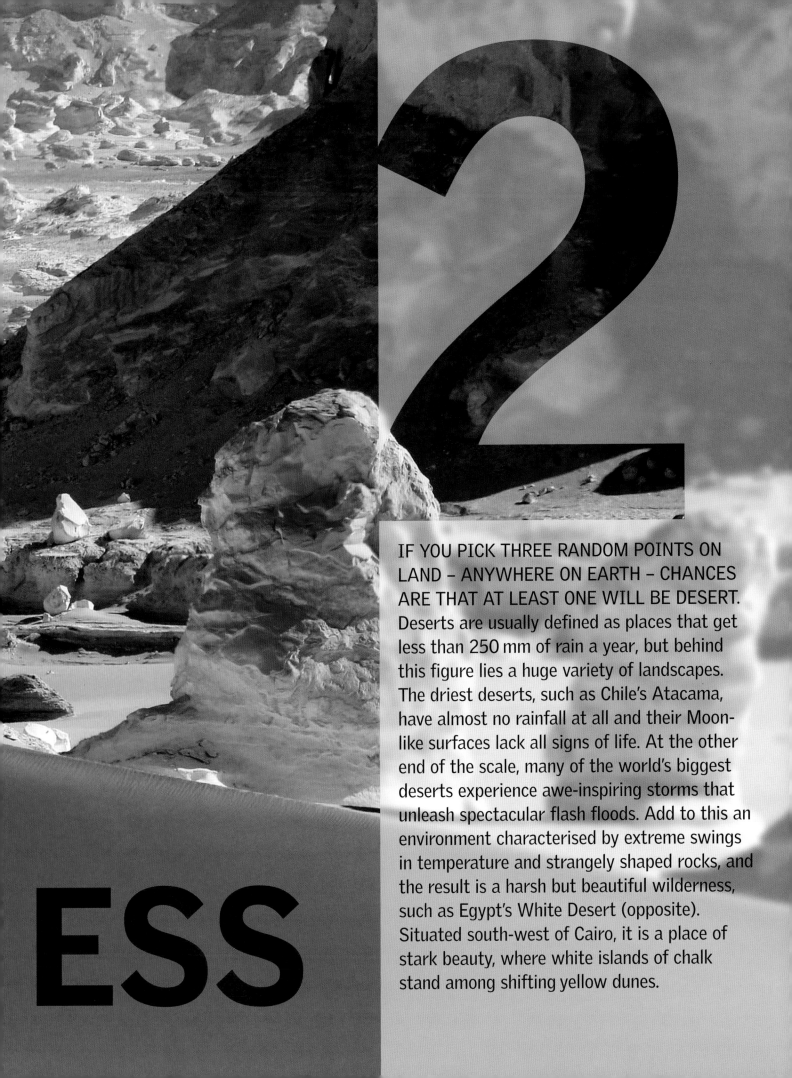

2

ESS

IF YOU PICK THREE RANDOM POINTS ON LAND – ANYWHERE ON EARTH – CHANCES ARE THAT AT LEAST ONE WILL BE DESERT. Deserts are usually defined as places that get less than 250 mm of rain a year, but behind this figure lies a huge variety of landscapes. The driest deserts, such as Chile's Atacama, have almost no rainfall at all and their Moon-like surfaces lack all signs of life. At the other end of the scale, many of the world's biggest deserts experience awe-inspiring storms that unleash spectacular flash floods. Add to this an environment characterised by extreme swings in temperature and strangely shaped rocks, and the result is a harsh but beautiful wilderness, such as Egypt's White Desert (opposite). Situated south-west of Cairo, it is a place of stark beauty, where white islands of chalk stand among shifting yellow dunes.

DESERT WEATHER

A DESERT IS THE LAST PLACE YOU MIGHT EXPECT TO GET COLD OR TO BE AT RISK FROM FLOODS. But deserts are places of extremes, where temperatures can tumble as well as soar, and where a whole year's rain can fall in a single day.

There is no such thing as a typical desert, although most of them share stark scenery. Starkest of all is the world's driest desert – the Atacama, which runs along the coast of northern Chile and into Peru. Throughout the Atacama's central zone there is not a single blade of vegetation, because no plant can survive in ground that is so absolutely dry. And without plants there is no soil, as there is nothing for microbes to break down.

Although the Atacama follows the coast, a less welcoming shoreline is hard to imagine. The grey coastal hills fall away into crumbling cliffs, with few safe spots to land. The only exceptions are a handful of narrow valleys, which wind across the desert like slender green ribbons carrying water from the Andes to the sea. The Atacama's first known inhabitants – a

A really big thunderstorm can shed over a million tonnes of water in less than an hour. With the hard parched ground unable to absorb the rainfall, water travels cross country like a wild animal on the loose.

people called the Chinchorro – lived near these river mouths at least 8000 years ago. They grew crops close to the running water, and used the nearby desert to preserve their dead, creating the world's earliest known mummified remains. Archaeologists have unearthed several hundred mummified men, women and children, buried in the dust-dry ground and facing out to sea.

The Atacama exists because an unusual mix of climatic conditions stops rainclouds forming. A cold offshore current, the Humboldt, cuts down the amount of moisture that can evaporate from the sea, while a permanent zone of high pressure keeps the skies clear. The combined influence of these features spreads along 500 km of the South American coast, and includes islands out at sea. In the centre of this zone there is no need for a weather forecast because there has been no rain here for at least 100 years.

The power of floods

Australia's Great Sandy Desert also has a shoreline – one of the longest and emptiest beaches in the world. But unlike the Atacama, this is a desert where it rains.

During the monsoon season, enormous thunderclouds can build up far inland, giving some parts of the desert up to 250 mm of rain a year. This sounds a lot, but in the scorching heat the water soon evaporates, leaving the ground almost as dry as before. The same is true of many deserts, from Africa to North America: the temperatures are high enough to evaporate more rain than actually falls.

But there is a catch. While a really big thunderstorm can shed over a million tonnes of water in less than an hour, evaporation can take days. What is more, thunderstorms are very localised, so the rain falls on a small area of ground. With the desert's drying system temporarily overloaded, and the hard, parched ground unable to absorb the rainfall, water travels cross country like a wild animal on the loose. The impact on the landscape can be devastating: as the water surges downhill, it picks up every rock particle below a certain size and washes it along. In a really big flash flood, the water lifts everything from tiny grains of quartz to boulders weighing as much as a car.

Eventually, the flow begins to slacken and the load is deposited. First to go are the biggest boulders, often dumped one by one. Next come smaller rocks, followed by gravel-sized particles, which can build up in layers over a

STORM BREWING Lightning strikes Arizona's Painted Desert. Such storms can send a deluge of water flooding across the parched landscape.

metre deep. Finally, the tiniest particles come to rest, often spreading out in thin sheets known as alluvial fans. Once the clouds clear, the Sun resumes its work and the water evaporates, leaving a changed landscape in its wake.

Flash floods are rare events in any one place, but the effect of such powerful surges of water builds up over time. To see what this can eventually lead to, look at the spectacular rock formations of the American West, which few places can match.

Carved cliffs

Thanks to innumerable films and adverts, the American West has become the epitome of desert scenery – a harshly beautiful world carved out of bare rock, sand and sunbaked clay. Much of this land receives less than 250 mm of rain a year, but signs of water and its power are everywhere. Seen from the air, streams of debris trace the path of flash floods, while alluvial fans spill out onto valley floors. In places like Arizona's Painted Desert,

FACTS

MANY DESERTS HAVE SURFACE TEMPERATURES
that are much higher than the surrounding air temperature. On July 15, 1972, the air temperature at Furnace Creek in Death Valley, USA, reached 53°C while the ground temperature was an extraordnary 94°C – easily hot enough to cook an egg.

ARICA IN NORTHERN CHILE has an average yearly rainfall of 0.76 mm. Rain falls mainly in isolated storms and in many years doesn't fall at all.

IN A FLASH FLOOD, WATER SPEEDS CAN REACH
20 m per second, which is very difficult to escape.

FACTS

water and wind have worked together to sculpt a chaotic vista of multicoloured hills and cliffs; in other areas, towering cliffs cast deep shadows in the setting sun.

These varied landscapes are all part of the Colorado Plateau, a high, semi-arid area stretching from the Rocky Mountains to the Sierra Nevada of California. Millions of years ago the region was much lower than it currently is, and seas alternately covered and receded from the area, depositing large quantities of sediment that formed layers of rock up to several kilometres deep. When the Rocky Mountains were formed, the plateau region was forced upwards. In the higher parts, much of the year's meagre moisture falls as winter snow. It is hard to imagine anything softer, but even this snowfall helps to create the desert's dramatic landscapes. When the snow thaws, the meltwater penetrates the rock beneath it, often freezing again when temperatures fall at night. The following day's heat may melt it again and so on. When water freezes it expands, and this cycle of freezing and thawing is more powerful than a jackhammer. The ice splits the rock apart, working its way deeper as it goes.

The combination of water, ice and flash floods has created some of the West's most stunning scenery: the flat-topped towers, or mesas, of Monument Valley. This part of the Colorado Plateau is topped by hard rock, which works like a waterproof shield. Beneath it is a deep layer of red sandstone – a softer rock

In terms of extreme winter cold, combined with remoteness and inaccessibility, the Gobi of Central Asia has no rivals. In winter, temperatures can drop to -30°C.

that is more easily penetrated by water and erodes more readily. Where water has managed to get in, the sandstone has broken up, creating cliffs and rocky debris that flash floods have carried away. Like the sea pounding the coast, water attacks these desert cliffs wherever and whenever it can. It turns headlands into peninsulas, and peninsulas into flat-topped islands. But these islands, or mesas, do not last forever. Each one eventually shrinks until it becomes a pillar, then a needle, before it finally disappears. Meanwhile, as the water and ice continue their work, more mesas are calved from the retreating cliffs to the west.

The world's hottest places

Deserts are easily the hottest places on Earth, but they are not usually found on the Equator, where the Sun is most direct. Many are thousands of kilometres away, in places where the Sun is lower in the sky. This may sound strange, but high temperatures do not guarantee dry conditions. On the Equator the air is full of moisture and soaks up a lot of incoming heat. This combination produces the world's tallest clouds, as well as almost daily

CAMEL TRAIN Bactrian camels are still used for transport in the Gobi Desert. A complete caravan can easily carry as much as a truck.

thunderstorms. On the edges of the tropics the air is clear and far drier, and far more of the Sun's heat travels through the atmosphere. As a result, subtropical deserts can warm up like ovens, while few places on the Equator reach more than 35°C.

Because temperature measurements are unreliable and difficult to compare, it is hard to establish the hottest point on Earth, but most meteorologists agree that the Sahara has several regions that are strong candidates. On September 13, 1922, El Aziziya in Algeria recorded a temperature of 57.7°C – the highest ever measured using a standard meteorological recording box, or Stevenson screen. One of the closest runners-up is Death Valley in the US states of California and Nevada. Here, the temperature at Furnace Creek has reached 54°C in summer, and it averages 37.8°C – equivalent to 100°F – on more than 125 days each year.

Although Death Valley is the hottest place in North America, there is some doubt about whether or not it holds the world record for sustained summer heat. Another strong contender is the town of Marble Bar, near Australia's north-western shoulder. The name may have a cool, refreshing ring to it, but Marble Bar is a place of fierce summer heat. In the 1920s, it recorded an unbroken run of 160 days on which temperatures reached 37.8°C. Unlike Death Valley, Marble Bar is inhabited, so it almost certainly wins the accolade of the world's hottest populated place.

Deserts that freeze

Marble Bar lies on the western edge of Australia's Great Sandy Desert – a part of the world that never experiences real cold. Even on winter nights the thermometer rarely falls below 10°C, and frosts are unknown. By comparison, winter in the Sahara is much more bracing: nights are often frosty, just as they are in the deserts of North America. But for extreme winter cold, combined with remoteness and inaccessibility, the Gobi Desert of Central Asia has no rivals. In winter, temperatures can drop to -30°C, making this desert as cold as some parts of Siberia.

The Gobi is huge: it covers more than 1 million km² of Central Asia north-east of the Himalayas. By the time the air reaches the region, most of the moisture has been wrung out of it, leaving only a few traces to nourish the desert's scanty plants. In the central area, most of the year's moisture falls not as rain but as dry, powdery snow, which is blown far and wide by the wind. Spring comes abruptly, and as the Asian landmass warms up, temperatures start to soar. By July the thermometer can reach 45°C, even though the Gobi is the most northerly of the world's great deserts.

Such a hostile environment is fraught with danger for humans; as well as the extremes of temperature and the possibility of running out of water, the constantly shifting sands make it easy to get lost. Yet for centuries people have crossed the deserts, often in pursuit of trade.

DESERT ART
In a dry desert climate, rocks often become covered with a layer of dark minerals, known as 'desert varnish'. The mineral layer builds up so slowly that even after thousands of years it is usually still thinner than a sheet of paper and can be scraped away with a stone to reveal the lighter rock beneath. In the past, desert people the world over used this technique to make a type of image known as a petroglyph. These Native American petroglyphs in the Petrified Forest National Park, Arizona, date from around AD 1000–1350. The purpose of the pictures is not known for sure; they may have had spiritual or ritualistic significance, or marked the seasons.

Desert crossings

Before the days of modern transport, merchants used established trade routes to transport goods across deserts, often on the backs of camels. One of the oldest and most famous is the Silk Road, which links China and Europe. Consisting of a network of routes, the Silk Road crossed the Gobi before continuing through Central Asia and the Middle East. Another set of routes run north to south across the Sahara, linking the countries bordering the southern Mediterranean with the rest of Africa. Even now, in both the Gobi and the Sahara, very few of these routes have a sealed surface. Instead, traffic makes its way across stony ground or shifting desert sands.

In the Gobi and the Sahara, some goods are now carried by trucks, but the camel trains have not completely disappeared. It is easy to see why: camels are extremely strong and resilient, with an instinctive footing on soft terrain. Their ability to go without water is legendary, but they can survive without food for several days as well. Unlike trucks, they are impervious to sandstorms, and they can also cope with extremely high temperatures without needing shade. During the winter camel trains work by day, but during the summer months caravans often travel by night, timing their journeys to make the best use of the Moon. In times gone by, journeys were often expressed in moons rather than in weeks or days.

SCULPTURES IN STONE

IN DESERTS THE NIGHTS ARE OFTEN CALM, but as soon as the Sun rises and warms the ground the wind begins to stir. Fierce and monotonous, wind can scour the ground for days or weeks at a time, often from the same direction. As well as making life difficult for animals, and setting people's nerves on edge, these winds slowly reshape objects in their path by blasting them with sand and grit, resulting in some of the strangest rock formations on Earth.

When the wind starts blowing, the smallest particles move first and travel furthest. Desert dust can be scooped up in enormous clouds, falling back to Earth hundreds or even thousands of kilometres away. Dust from the Sahara frequently gets blown to southern Europe by a wind known as the sirocco, and on occasions it can reach as far as the British Isles. In California, the Santa Ana wind blows dust and sand out to sea, often fanning forest fires. Both these winds carry the desert heat – in California, the temperature can rise by 10°C in as many hours.

In time, the wind blows away all of the finest particles of dust, revealing whatever is hidden

EGYPT

BALANCING ACT In Egypt's White Desert, eroded balls of rock stand on slender pillars of chalk. Differential weathering by the wind has eroded the softer particles, leaving the harder rock behind in precarious configurations.

ARGENTINA

UTAH

CALIFORNIA

BOWLING ALLEY These natural rock spheres in Argentina's Ischigualasto Park formed underwater and were later buried by sand. The wind revealed them when it blew the sand away.

ROCK TOADSTOOLS Utah's white Wahweap Hoodoos have been sculpted by rain. Each one consists of a pillar of soft white sandstone topped by a much harder, dark sandstone 'hat'.

SLIDING STONES In Death Valley's Racetrack Playa, moving boulders have left tracks in drying clay. Many geologists believe that flash floods cause the boulders to slide.

underneath. In many flat parts of the Sahara, wind has uncovered huge plains of closely set pebbles, which were washed into their present positions long ago, when the climate was much wetter than today. These pebbles make up a desert pavement, or 'reg', which is notoriously uncomfortable for travellers. Australia also has large swathes of this kind of pebble desert surface. Known locally as a 'gibber', the pavement is often just one stone thick, and is easily scarred by vehicle tracks because there are few plants to cover any tracks and little rain to wash them away.

When a dust storm strikes, most living things take cover and wait until the storm has moved on. Even vehicles are brought to a halt as dust finds its way through filters and into drivers'

ears and eyes. But wind can also work less visibly, through a process that can be felt closer to the ground. Called saltation, it happens when the wind is strong enough to make particles of grit 'hop' into the air. The height of each hop is typically about a metre, while the distance travelled can be five times that or more. Once one hop is over, the next one begins.

On exposed skin, saltation feels like being blasted by a gritty hair-drier, which is why it makes good sense to keep arms and legs well covered up when travelling through the desert. Humans and other animals can take refuge from saltation, but inanimate obstacles – such as rocky outcrops – suffer this invisible bombardment day after day. The effect is like a tiny mason with a chisel, slowly chipping into a piece of stone. If it carries on long enough, saltation creates rocks that are perched on narrow 'waists'. The waists keep shrinking until they finally give way and the uppermost lump of rock tumbles to the desert floor.

THE WORK OF WIND AND RAIN

IN DESERTS, THE WIND CAN WORK UNAIDED, BUT IT IS OFTEN HELPED BY RAIN. Together, they can create all kinds of geological spectacles, from giant perched rocks to badlands – eerie landscapes where little moves and almost nothing grows.

Wind and water can take thousands of years to carve a perched rock out of sandstone, even though the rock is fairly soft with convenient layers, or 'strata', that the forces of erosion can exploit. Granite is a much tougher nut to crack. Unlike sandstone, it is made of interlocking crystals and is a byword for hardness and strength. Several hours are needed to saw through a slab of granite, so it's not a rock you would expect to erode with any ease. But all over the world, from deserts to mountains, granite outcrops are famous for their fantastic size and curvaceous shapes. Dartmoor, in south-west England, has granite tors some of which look like piles of plates, while on Kangaroo Island, off Australia's southern coast, a collection of granite monoliths look like 1950s sculptures, with curving bodies perched on angular elbows and knees. Africa is a particularly good place to see this natural art: South Africa and Zimbabwe have some of the biggest examples in the world. Many of the monoliths weigh thousands of tonnes, and are so big and smooth they are impossible to scale without climbing gear.

Most kinds of granite are hard enough to scratch glass, so how do they get their rounded shape? The answer lies in the distant past, when the granite formed. Granite is an igneous rock, created by volcanic heat. As it cools and turns solid, it often shrinks and develops deep cracks. These cracks run in three dimensions, dividing the rock into giant blocks. If surface water penetrates these cracks, it introduces acids from the soil and rock overlying the granite. Granite is hard, but it is vulnerable to acids so erosion starts while the rock is underground. Where erosion removes overlying layers, the granite becomes exposed, and within a relatively short time the cracks start to widen and the curvaceous contours form.

> When erosion gets to work on clay, the result is a harsh kind of desert terrain. In all directions, low rounded hills are separated by steep-sided ravines, with very few plants and almost no soil.

Good-for-nothing lands

When erosion gets to work on clay rather than rock, the result is a particularly harsh kind of desert terrain. In all directions, low rounded hills are separated by steep-sided ravines, with very few plants and almost no soil. The clay is baked as hard as pottery when it is dry, but if rain falls, the ground can turn as slippery as an icy road. In North America, European settlers called these areas 'badlands' because they were no good for grazing or farming, and the name has stuck.

Avoided by people and wildlife, badlands have a strange and unsettling atmosphere. But among these clay hills, surprises are sometimes hidden away. Arizona's Painted Desert is one of the world's most spectacularly colourful badlands, thanks to bands of organic remains and minerals that were laid down in the distant past. Revealed by erosion, these horizontal bands are particularly eyecatching early and late in the day, when the Sun is low. Some badlands have relics of a much more fertile past: from time to time, erosion reveals spectacular fossils, including the remains of dinosaurs. North America's badlands include some of the best dinosaur-hunting terrain in the world – a treasure-trove of evolution preserved in eroding clay.

CAREFULLY POISED Perched rocks look dangerous, but erosion makes them settle and shrink instead of toppling over.

ANCIENT ART *Among the Nazca Lines is a 50 m long spider and a human figure known as the owl-man. Although the lines etched into the desert floor are shallow, they have not been worn away by erosion.*

The past preserved

In most parts of the world, when humans move out nature soon takes over. Houses disappear among trees, and farmland is overrun. Given enough time, entire cities are swallowed up – something that has happened more than once in different parts of the world. Deserts are different. Because they have so few plants, human artefacts last far longer than they would do in places with wetter climates. This legacy includes ancient structures, such as the pyramids of Egypt, as well as some enigmatic works of art, as seen in the Nazca Lines of Peru.

The Great Pyramid of Giza, on the edge of the Sahara's Western Desert, was built over 4500 years ago. Its outer casing has largely disappeared, stolen for use in later projects, but apart from this loss the pyramid has survived almost intact. If the same structure had been built in the tropics, or in the damp climate of northern Europe, rain would have attacked its limestone blocks and trees would have taken root in the cracks. Although the pyramid would probably have survived, it would not be in as good a state of preservation.

The giant drawings traced out on the surface of Peru's Nazca Desert, and known as the Nazca Lines, were created over a period of about 500 years, starting around AD 200. The lines were made by clearing stones from the surface of the desert to reveal the lighter bedrock beneath. The result of all this work is best appreciated from the air: as well as parallel lines and geometric patterns, there are animals such as a monkey and a snake dozens of metres across. No one knows why the Nazca people created these figures, but we do know how they have been preserved for so long. The Nazca Desert borders the Atacama, and shares the same dry climate. It is also a desert with very little wind. The absence of water and wind – the two major causes of erosion – is why the Nazca Lines have lasted down the centuries, even though many of them are less than 20 cm deep.

PERMANENT WATER, FLOURISHING VEGETATION, FROGS, FISH AND FRESHWATER SNAILS are not what spring to mind when you think about a desert, but they are found at many oases. Thanks to natural underground reservoirs, oases provide a lush contrast to their arid surroundings.

The ancient Egyptians gave us the word 'oasis' – they started farming some of these islands in the desert more than 8000 years ago. Oases can be just a few hundred metres across, but Egypt has five much larger ones that were settled even before the days of the pharaohs. The largest, at El-Fayoum, is not far from the Nile, but the most remote, at Siwa, is over 500 km further west, in the vast emptiness of the Sahara. Even today, Siwa is difficult to reach, and in the days before modern transport its inhabitants had little day-to-day contact with the outside world. This sealed-off quality makes oases special, quite apart from water and greenery set in such barren land.

Oases are found in cold deserts as well as hot. The water comes from underground reservoirs, called aquifers, which consist of a honeycomb structure of connected spaces inside porous rock. The scale of these water reserves is enormous. For example, the great Nubian Sandstone Aquifer extends beneath most of Egypt and into neighbouring parts of Libya, Chad and Sudan. This single aquifer contains enough

Compared to rainwater, the water in oases is extremely old. In some cold deserts – such as the Gobi – it comes from ice-age glaciers, which melted over 12 000 years ago.

OASES

FOSSIL WATER The still waters in this Saharan oasis come from rain that fell thousands of years ago and then travelled underground.

OASIS RESIDENTS Most weaver birds nest in groups. These ones have built their nests high in a date palm in an African oasis.

water to drown the Great Pyramid along with the whole of the rest of Egypt. However, except where the water comes to the surface at oases, all of it lies hidden beneath the Sahara's rock and sand.

Fit to drink

Compared to rainwater, the water in oases is extremely old. In some cold deserts – such as the Gobi – it comes from Ice Age glaciers, which melted over 12 000 years ago. What is more, oasis water often comes from far away. Its journey usually begins on mountains, and it can then travel hundreds or thousands of miles underground before it re-emerges at the surface. During this subterranean journey, the water often picks up mineral salts. A small amount gives it a slight mineral tang, but a high dose can make oasis water undrinkable – for humans at least. Many desert animals can survive on water that is not only mineral-laden, but as warm as a shower. These salt-tolerant creatures include insect grubs, and even water snails.

Some of the smallest and strangest salt-laden oases are in South Australia, on the edge of the Great Artesian Basin. This huge aquifer drains water away from the mountains of eastern Australia and into the continent's dry interior. Some of this water eventually emerges in South Australia, in a line of desert springs that stretches for more than 500 km. The Mound Springs National Park straddles a section of this line in the parched Australian bush far to the north of Adelaide. The flat, Moon-like landscape is dotted with mounds that look like miniature volcanoes up to 30 m high. Each mound marks a point where springwater comes out of the ground, leaving a crust of minerals as it evaporates into the air.

A bright green fringe of algae and low-growing desert plants surround the flowing springs. But these mini-oases have a limited lifetime; as they age, the flow starts to subside. Finally, the water is choked off and the spring dries up. When this happens, the algae and plants die and the mound community becomes extinct.

Oasis animals

In deserts, water is a magnet for animals of all kinds. The most common visitors are birds – among the finest of nature's navigators. For swallows and other long-distance migrants, oases are important stopover points during long desert crossings. Instead of finding oases by accident, some of these birds inherit a navigation map that guides them to water along their route. In the deserts of Africa and Asia, male sandgrouse are daily visitors, flying in every morning to collect water for their young. Their breast feathers work like sponges, soaking up water, which they carry back to their nests. Many oases also have their own resident bird life, with finches and weaver birds featuring high on the list. Nesting in trees overhanging water, they chatter noisily at dawn and dusk.

When darkness falls, the air is sometimes filled with the sound of croaking frogs – a bizarre soundtrack in the desert, but many oases are full of creatures that live in or near water. These include mosquitoes and dragonflies, which grow up in water, and some of the world's smallest and most localised freshwater fish. One of them, the Elizabeth Springs goby, lives in a single group of mound-springs in Queensland, Australia. Its total habitat covers about 15 000 m² – twice the size of a football pitch. But even this looks generous compared with the living space used by the Devil's Hole pupfish from Nevada. The entire species, numbering between 200 and 500 fish, live and

FACTS

ONE OF THE HIGHEST OASES IS SAN PEDRO DE ATACAMA, in Chile. It lies on a plateau 2400 m high, surrounded by the Atacama Desert. The water naturally contains high levels of arsenic, yet people have lived in the region for thousands of years without apparent ill effect. A water-treatment plant now removes the arsenic.

LAS VEGAS is built on the site of an oasis in the Mojave Desert. The oasis was discovered by European settlers in the early 1800s.

THE GREAT ARTESIAN BASIN OF AUSTRALIA extends beneath more than a fifth of the continent.

FACTS

RIVER OASIS *Seen from the air, the Loa River cuts through the bone-dry hills of the Atacama Desert on its journey to the ocean.*

Neither of these animals could have crossed the desert to reach water, and it is just as certain that they did not get there with human help. Instead, they are evidence that the Sahara's climate has slowly dried. Grasslands and wetlands have been replaced by desert, and apart from oases, surface water has disappeared. The hippo has long gone, after fighting a battle against both the changing climate and human hunters. The crocodile still hangs on, clinging to life where lakes and pools near seasonal rivers provide enough water for it to survive.

A river runs through

Most people's idea of an oasis is something like an island, an isolated patch of green in the parched desert. But not all oases are like this. Where rivers flow through dry surroundings, they create ribbon-like oases that can be thousands of miles long. The Nile is the biggest desert river in the world. It collects all its water in the highlands of East Africa, and then flows through the Sahara like a geological feature that has lost its way. Desert rivers also include the Tigris and Euphrates in the Middle East, the Darling in Australia, and the Colorado in the United States. In South America, some rivers even cross the Atacama – the driest desert of all.

Seen from the air, desert rivers stand out like vivid green veins. But even where there is no surface water most of the time, desert plants can form long, branching, straggling lines. These lines spread out like fingers across the desert floor, reaching up into valleys from the lower ground. They mark the path that water follows during rare flash floods, and plants grow along

breed in a single, water-filled cavern in Death Valley. Its living space measures less than 20 m², one of the tiniest habitats of any vertebrate on Earth.

Survivors of a watery past

Frogs and fish reach oases as eggs carried on the legs of birds, but in some parts of the world remote oases are home to much larger water animals that cannot travel in this way. For example, a small group of Nile crocodiles was recently discovered in the Tagant Hills of Mauritania, on the southern edge of the Sahara – a region where there is no flowing water. Nile crocodiles are also found on the Ennedi Plateau in northern Chad. Further back in time, rock paintings show people hunting hippos in the centre of the Sahara over 4000 years ago.

these gulleys and valleys because there is slightly more moisture here than in the surrounding ground. In the Middle East, these valleys are known as wadis – a word that is often applied to other deserts as well. Palm trees often grow in wadis, and so do oleanders – evergreen shrubs with bright pink flowers from North Africa, Asia and the Middle East.

Wadis provide obvious advantages for plants, but there is a big minus point, too. When it does rain, flood water rushes down the wadi in full force and batters plants with the pieces of rock, grit and sand that it has picked up along the way; anything that is not very tough risks being uprooted or snapped off and swept away. Palm trees cope by having tough trunks, but oleanders use a different tactic. If they get uprooted and buried again, they resprout – sometimes hundreds of metres away.

ONCE THE LEAST POPULATED AND MOST

ISOLATED OASIS IN EGYPT'S WESTERN DESERT, THE FARAFRA OASIS IS TODAY EXPANDING FAST. The Farafra Oasis lies in the Western Desert's deepest and second-largest depression, which also includes Egypt's White Desert. Like Egypt's other oases, Farafra was known in the days of the pharaohs, although the ancient Egyptians were almost certainly not the first people to discover it. Humans probably roamed this part of the Sahara thousands of years ago, when the climate was wetter than it is today. As the climate dried, people settled in the remaining patches of savannah, surrounded and isolated by the encroaching sand. For thousands of years just a few natural springs – some gushing warm, mineral-rich water – reached the surface at Farafra so the oasis remained small. Bedouin farmers raised sheep and goats there and grew fruit such as dates and olives.

In the second half of the 20th century all this changed. Exploration of the Nubian Sandstone Aquifer revealed large reserves of water beneath the Farafra Depression. In addition, water from the Nile Valley and the other Western Desert oases drains into the depression, constantly replenishing the aquifer. The Egyptian government responded by drilling wells for irrigation – some up to 1200 m deep – and building a series of new villages in an ambitious scheme to develop the oasis and increase food production there. In just a few years the area under cultivation expanded from 1214 to 8903 hectares, and the population rose from 5000 – in Qasr Farafra, once the only village in the oasis – to 15 000 as people moved from Cairo and the Delta region to start a new life farming in the rapidly greening desert.

VITAL STATISTICS

LOCATION: Western Egypt
SIZE: 10 000 km²
POPULATION: 15 000
CLIMATE: Typical annual rainfall is zero. Maximum temperature is 45°C, dropping to freezing on winter nights
MAIN SETTLEMENT: Qasr Farafra
CROPS: Dates, olives, wheat, rice, beans, apricots

FARAFRA

OASIS

GHOSTS AND GEMS

DESERTS ARE SOME OF THE BEST PLACES ON EARTH FOR FINDING MINERALS AND PRECIOUS STONES. People have made their fortunes – and also lost them – extracting minerals from the desert. Today, eerie ghost towns mark regions where once booming mineral extraction went into rapid decline.

The biggest of the mineral rushes started in the Atacama Desert in the early 1800s, and involved a mineral salt called sodium nitrate or 'Chile saltpetre'. This salt was – and still is – an important ingredient for making explosives and fertilisers, but because it dissolves easily, it is rarely found in places where it rains. In the Atacama, of course, rain is

SANDS OF TIME A rusting steam train at Humberstone in the Atacama Desert recalls an era when the region had a thriving nitrate industry. Inset: Sand has half-filled a hospital building at Kollmannskuppe, Namibia – a former bustling diamond-mining town.

not a problem, and prospectors found huge quantities of sodium nitrate waiting to be mined. Within a few decades, a great nitrate industry was underway. By the mid-1800s, thousands of tonnes of nitrate were being exported from seaports on the desert coast. As the boom gained momentum, entire towns began to spring up in the desert, serviced by narrow-gauge railways that carried the nitrate ore. The miners themselves lived in a strange world that was literally without any clouds in the sky. The only green plants they saw were the result of irrigation, and water was something that only ever came out of a tank.

Boom and bust

Whenever a crucial commodity is at stake, political tensions are never far away. In the late 1870s, such tensions erupted into open warfare between Bolivia and Chile over the northern part of the Atacama, and its rich nitrate mines. Peru also entered the conflict, which was fought both on land and at sea from 1879 to 1883. By the time the war finished, Chile had gained Bolivia's entire share of the desert, and with it that nation's only access to the coast. It is a loss that Bolivians still feel keenly to this day.

The nitrate boom continued for several further decades, but history eventually ended it in a quite unexpected way. In the early 1900s, German chemists perfected a way of making ammonia – a substance that can replace sodium nitrate in many chemical reactions. Suddenly, the bottom dropped out of the Chilean saltpetre trade, with its high shipping costs and distant mines. One by one the mining towns closed, and their workers moved elsewhere. Several of the abandoned towns are now classified as World Heritage Sites in recognition of their remarkable history in a unique part of the world.

DESERT ROSE This natural crystal formation is made of the mineral gypsum. In deserts, where the mineral is formed by the evaporation of rising groundwater, it occurs in the form of petals, creating the appearance of flowers.

The lure of precious stones

Deserts provide all kinds of minerals, but their most valuable wealth comes from precious metals and gems. Some of the world's biggest gold nuggets have been found in desert terrain. Opals are another desert speciality, with many originating from the desert mining town of Coober Pedy in South Australia. Diamonds also turn up in the desert, deposited there in ancient river sediments. The Namib Desert, along southern Africa's Skeleton Coast, is the location of some of the world's remotest diamond mines. The town of Kollmannskuppe, founded in the early 1900s, was once home to over 700 inhabitants, with a hospital and even a casino. But diamond production dwindled, and richer deposits were found offshore. Within just 40 years, the town was abandoned. Today, its buildings lie empty, and partly engulfed by the desert sand.

DESERTS ON THE MOVE

DESERTS DON'T HAVE FIXED BOUNDARIES – instead, they shift with changes in weather patterns. For people who live on the fringes of deserts, the threat of being engulfed is never far away. Of all the world's deserts, the Sahara is one of those most affected by climate change. Thousands of years ago, enough rain fell here to carve out river channels, but these have long since dried up and filled with sand. Lake Chad, on the southern edge of the Sahara, is all that remains of a vast inland sea that, around 6000 years ago, covered an estimated 400 000 km². Fossilised pollen shows that the Sahara's central mountains used to be covered with oaks and cedars, while rock paintings show that the southern edge of the desert was home to elephants, rhinos and giraffes only 3000 years ago – hard to imagine, looking at the barren desert that exists today.

Still further back in time, at the height of the last ice-age, the Sahara was even larger and drier than it is now. It seems that over thousands of years the Sahara's climate has swung to and fro, and the desert has expanded and contracted, leaving evidence that expert eyes can spot.

Man-made climate change

Until recently in the Earth's history, changes like these were triggered by natural climate change. But since the start of farming, about 10 000 years ago, humans have inadvertently helped deserts to spread, and encouraged new ones to form. One way that this happens is by raising more animals than the land can support. This strips the land of its plant cover, exposing the soil to the drying effects of sunshine and wind. The dried-out soil is easily blown away, permanently destroying the plant cover. Intense cultivation can have the same effect, particularly if the land is left bare at dry times of the year.

Deserts can also be created where water is brought to the surface. A single well can start a desert in miniature as animals flock to it to drink. On a bigger scale, even slightly salty groundwater used in irrigation contaminates the soil over time because the salt concentration builds up as the water evaporates in the sun.

Salty soil – or salination – turned some of the world's earliest farmland into desert in the Middle East, and the process is still at work. The problem is serious in Australia, where farmers have cut down forests to clear land for wheat. Australia's native gum trees are salt-tolerant, but with the trees gone the water table has risen, bringing salty groundwater with it. The result is salt-damaged land that will turn into desert unless the salt can be flushed out.

PINCER MOVEMENT Crescent-shaped dunes – or barchans – threaten fields in an Egyptian oasis. Dunes like this may be hundreds of years old.

DAILY RITUAL Water shortage is a problem on the edge of deserts. In some places, water is being pumped from the underground aquifer faster than it is replaced.

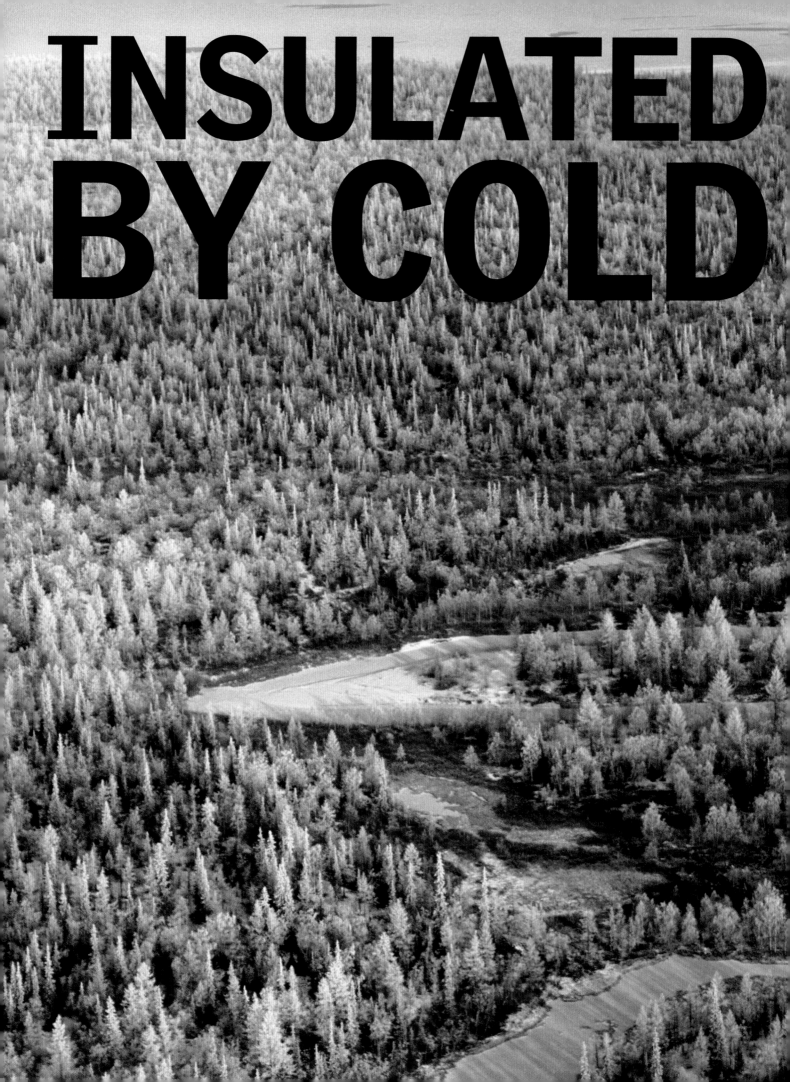

INSULATED
BY COLD

3

THE WORLD'S COLDEST PLACES DO NOT LIE DIRECTLY AT THE POLES. The lowest temperature officially recorded was −89.2°C at a research station in the Antarctic, almost 1300 km from the South Pole. In the Northern Hemisphere, Siberia (left) has the world's coldest permanently inhabited places: the extreme continental climate here can produce a difference between winter and summer temperatures of nearly 110°C. In these regions, winter may lock entire landscapes under ice and snow for six months of the year. As a result of such conditions, the far northern parts of Europe, Asia and North America include some of Earth's wildest places, rarely built on and never farmed. For the few communities living there, the winter freeze-up brings some advantages, such as the possibility of constructing 'ice roads' across frozen lakes.

REINDEER HERDING For centuries, people living in Arctic regions of Europe and Asia have herded reindeer for their meat, milk and hides. Unlike fully domesticated animals, reindeer wander freely. Nomadic herders, such as the Nenets of western Siberia, follow the animals in their annual migrations and have never attempted to raise them in captivity.

POLE of COLD

SOME TOWNS ARE PROUD OF THEIR HISTORY, ARCHITECTURE OR LEAFY PARKS. In north-eastern Siberia, the people of Verkhoyansk are stoically proud of their bitter climate. 'Summer always comes as a shock to us,' the mayor tells a visiting reporter. 'This is a really cold place most of the time. Very, very cold.'

Verkhoyansk is probably the coldest inhabited place on Earth. In 1892 the thermometer fell to –69.8°C, setting a record that has remained unbeaten ever since. Another Siberian town,

Oymyakon, registered –71.2°C in 1926, but differences in measuring techniques mean that Verkhoyansk is probably the colder of the two by a fraction of a degree. The two towns have a number of features in common. Both are in the Russian far east. Both are in broad river valleys, flanked by high mountains. Strangest of all, both are hundreds of miles from the North Pole.

In the Southern Hemisphere, too, there is a mismatch between the geographical pole and the 'pole of cold'. The world's coldest place is Vostok Station, a Russian research station in

Life in the freezer

This incredible temperature variation has far-reaching effects on daily life. During the summer, the surface of the ground briefly thaws, but beneath this is a frozen layer – known as permafrost – that remains rock-hard. Growing food is such a challenge here that few people even try. Instead, life is traditionally based on reindeer herding, fishing and fur-trapping – anything else has to be brought in from outside. Food is frozen simply by putting it in a cellar: even in summer, there is no need for a fridge.

Keeping warm in winter is an endurance test that can last seven months or more. Most of Verkhoyansk's houses are heated by wood, often the biggest item in a family budget. A trip outside needs an almost complete cover-up to avoid frostbite. In the intense cold, oil turns waxy, plastic becomes brittle and rubber boots can crack into pieces. Water is cut from the nearby Yana River in blocks, and stacked outside. In summer, when the river melts, the whole of Verkoyansk seems to be working round the clock, preparing for the next winter, never more than a few weeks away.

ICED ANGELICA Frost encrusts an angelica plant growing by a river in Iceland. In regions where cultivation is difficult, edible wild plants have traditionally been a valuable food source. Angelica was eaten as a vegetable, and the Sami of northern Scandinavia used to mix it with reindeer milk.

Antarctica, nearly 1300 km from the South Pole. The lowest temperature ever recorded at Vostok is –89.2°C – a record for anywhere on Earth – while the record for the South Pole is –82.8°C. The colder temperature at Vostok is due to two factors: it is higher than the South Pole, and it is nearer to the centre of the Greater Antarctic ice sheet, the world's biggest body of ice.

In Siberia, the ice sheet melted at the end of the last ice age about 10 000 years ago. Instead, the region owes its extreme climate to its position in the north-east of the world's biggest continent, far from the moderating influence of the oceans. In summer, high pressure air often settles over the area, trapping warm air and sending the thermometer soaring, while in winter, cold air slides down from the Arctic and has exactly the opposite effect. The coldest air settles at the bottom of river valleys, giving Verkhoyansk an annual temperature range of nearly 110°C.

FROZEN CHALLENGE *Hanging onto two ice picks, a climber scales a series of frozen waterfalls in the Canadian Rockies.*

FROZEN IN MOTION

IN THE CANADIAN ARCTIC, THE MACKENZIE RIVER STARTS TO FREEZE OVER IN OCTOBER. Ice first creates fringes around rocky islands and along the river's banks, then it reaches farther out into the water. Next, tiny ice crystals form in the main body of the river. This 'frazil' ice makes the water slushy and gives the surface an oily sheen. In the final stage, the frazil becomes rounded slabs, called 'ice pans', which collide with one another and freeze together. Once this has happened, the 1700 km Mackenzie stays frozen until May. Beneath the ice, the river keeps on flowing, but its water is sealed away.

Flowing and still water respond to the cold in different ways. When the temperature falls below zero, ponds and lakes soon start to freeze, but moving water takes longer, with results that can be both spectacularly beautiful and highly dangerous. Frazil ice can be treacherous, swirling around and piling up against anything in its path, such as rocks or fallen trees. Frazil also sticks to itself, so that a small amount can quickly grow, turning into a giant ice dam, which may completely block a river, like a cork in a hose. Eventually, the dam gives way and a huge surge of water erupts downstream, sweeping aside anything in its way.

Falls of ice

Even more spectacular than frozen rivers – and much rarer – are frozen waterfalls, which are among the most stunning sights created by extreme winter cold. For an entire waterfall to freeze,

BURSTING POINT *A frozen river in eastern Siberia bulges like a defective pipe. An ice dam has blocked its flow, but if the pressure continues the dam will burst, releasing a deluge of pent-up water downhill.*

the ideal combination is a slow water flow with sharp night-time cold. In Iceland, several waterfalls come close to freezing solid in winter because the cold reduces their flow. Of these, the most famous is the Gullfoss, where the River Hvíta makes a sharp left turn before plunging into a slot-like gorge. In winter, it becomes a staircase of milky-coloured ice, blanketed by snow. Yet even in the coldest weather, a few narrow torrents still pour over its edge.

A dramatic example of a frozen waterfall occurred in 1848, when an ice jam briefly blocked the Niagara Falls in North America. In normal winters, the volume of water on the move at Niagara is too vast for the falls to freeze – although their mist and spray often does, forming mounds of ice up to 15 m thick. But in 1848 the ice jam cut the water flow to a trickle. The falls turned into a vast, broken curtain of ice, staying this way for several hours, until the jam cleared and the flow resumed.

Giant icicles

The best place to find frozen waterfalls on a regular basis is high up – in ice-climbing terrain. The Alps have well-known ice-climbs, as do the Himalayas, but among climbers the Canadian Rockies are generally regarded as having the world's best frozen falls. Here, glaciers in the last ice age gouged out U-shaped valleys with near-vertical sides. In summer, meltwater feeds

streams that trickle over their rocky ledges, and in winter these waterfalls turn into cascades of ice.

With their sharply pointed pinnacles, the frozen falls look fragile, but they are a world away from the icicles that form around the edges of roofs. Individual pinnacles can be more than 10 m long and weigh many tonnes. Some hang freely in empty space, while others seem to pour down the rock face, even though they are locked in place. Every year, they form in the same locations, although their exact shape is never the same.

For ice-climbers, scaling the vertical ice of frozen falls is the ultimate challenge. They use lightweight ice picks to create handholds, while special boots fitted with forward-pointing teeth provide footholds. In good conditions, ice is surprisingly tough, and holds just 2 cm deep are easily strong enough to support a climber's weight. But free-hanging ice is unpredictable. A sudden change in temperature can make a climb that was safe one week extremely hazardous the next, the ice collapsing when it takes a climber's weight.

Because of the way ice forms in waterfalls, climbers are constantly moving up a series of overhangs. As a result, they often have a good view of the drop below, but little idea of what lies immediately above. The reward comes from achieving the almost impossible – and living to tell the tale.

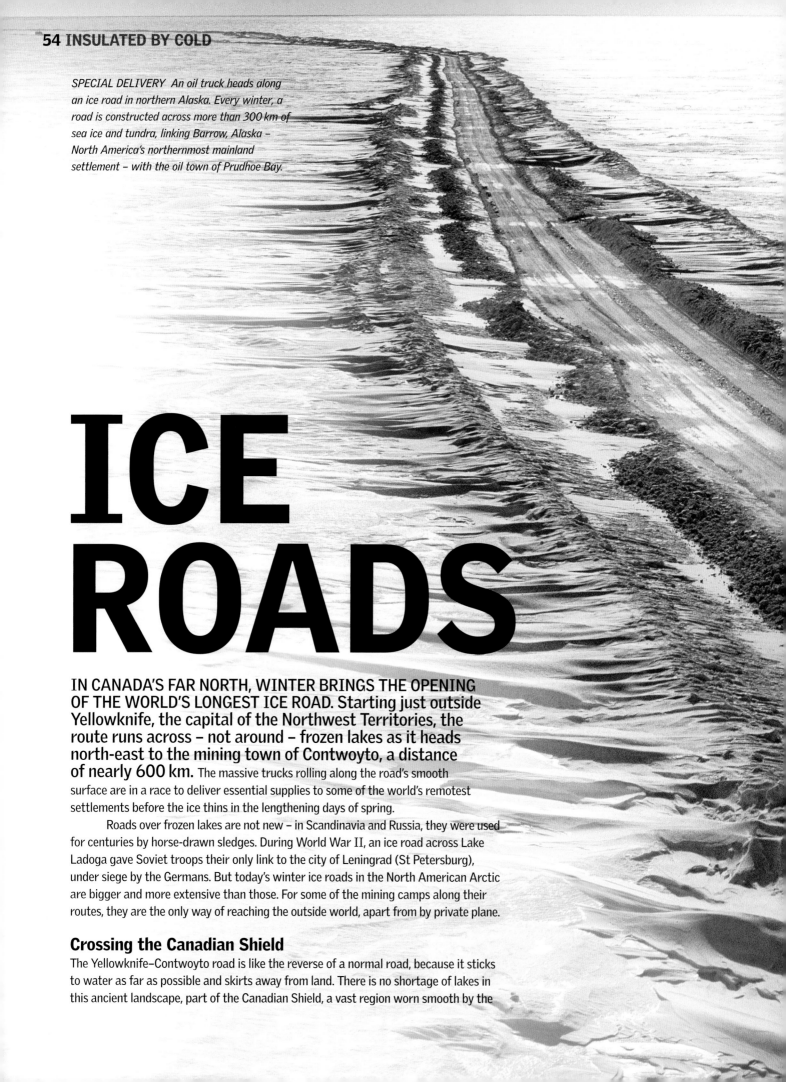

SPECIAL DELIVERY An oil truck heads along an ice road in northern Alaska. Every winter, a road is constructed across more than 300 km of sea ice and tundra, linking Barrow, Alaska – North America's northernmost mainland settlement – with the oil town of Prudhoe Bay.

ICE ROADS

IN CANADA'S FAR NORTH, WINTER BRINGS THE OPENING OF THE WORLD'S LONGEST ICE ROAD. Starting just outside Yellowknife, the capital of the Northwest Territories, the route runs across – not around – frozen lakes as it heads north-east to the mining town of Contwoyto, a distance of nearly 600 km. The massive trucks rolling along the road's smooth surface are in a race to deliver essential supplies to some of the world's remotest settlements before the ice thins in the lengthening days of spring.

Roads over frozen lakes are not new – in Scandinavia and Russia, they were used for centuries by horse-drawn sledges. During World War II, an ice road across Lake Ladoga gave Soviet troops their only link to the city of Leningrad (St Petersburg), under siege by the Germans. But today's winter ice roads in the North American Arctic are bigger and more extensive than those. For some of the mining camps along their routes, they are the only way of reaching the outside world, apart from by private plane.

Crossing the Canadian Shield

The Yellowknife–Contwoyto road is like the reverse of a normal road, because it sticks to water as far as possible and skirts away from land. There is no shortage of lakes in this ancient landscape, part of the Canadian Shield, a vast region worn smooth by the power of ice-age glaciers, which also scraped away most of the soil. As the climate warmed at the end of the last ice age, the glaciers retreated, leaving hundreds of thousands of hollows, which became freshwater lakes – many of them small, but some enormous. Great Slave Lake is nearly 500 km long and more than 600 m deep. Great Bear Lake, near the Arctic Ocean, covers in excess of 30 000 km² and is the seventh-largest lake in the world. In winter, many of the lakes are covered with more than a metre of ice, topped by up to 30 cm of snow.

The Contwoyto ice road usually opens in late January, once engineers have verified an ice depth of at least 70 cm. The route is ploughed to clear it of snow and to smoothe the surface – this also marks the road for drivers, an important safety feature for journeys in weak winter daylight. Because snow works like an insulating blanket, shielding the relatively warm lake water from the cold Arctic air, clearing the snow also helps to thicken the ice. With the snow removed, the water in contact with the ice gets an extra chilling and the ice builds up. In an average year, the Contwoyto ice road stays open until early April – well before the spring thaw makes it unsafe. The road's extra-thick ice is usually the last to melt away.

When the ice is thickest, towards late February, it can safely bear a truck and its cargo with a combined weight of 60 tonnes. The ice creaks as trucks drive over it, and cracks sometimes appear, but these reseal themselves in seconds, like an elastic skin. On the rare occasions when trucks have sunk, the process has been slow enough for drivers to call for help before scrambling out of their cabs – so far not a single driver has been lost. Safety measures are stringent. The speed limit for laden vehicles is 25 km/h, partly to cut down the risk of collisions, and partly to reduce the risk of pressure waves being generated in the water as a truck rolls over the ice above it. These are not a problem in deep water, but in water near a lake's shore, they can bounce upwards from the shallow bed. If a vehicle is moving too quickly, the water bursts upwards through pressure cracks, which then have to be resealed.

FACTS

LAKE ICE WAS HARVESTED FOR SALE BEFORE THE invention of refrigerators. Ice cut from lakes and rivers in New England was packed in straw for insulation and shipped as far afield as India.

A 10 CM LAYER of ice is usually safe to walk on. A snowmobile needs ice that is about 15 cm thick, while a layer 30 cm thick will support a car.

THE ICE DEPTH OVER NORTH AMERICA'S GREAT Lakes can be more than 80 cm. **FACTS**

NORTH AMERICA'S CASCADE RANGE, RUNNING PARALLEL WITH THE PACIFIC COAST, SCOOPS MOST WORLD RECORDS FOR SNOW. The Cascades' annual snowfall can be more than 250 times the amount falling near the poles. Storms pile the snow so deep that it could bury a family home. These colossal falls are not simply due to the cold; they are a spectacular by-product of the mountains' position. Rising close to the Pacific coast of Canada and the USA, the Cascades get a massive helping of snow's chief ingredient – moisture-laden air. As the prevailing westerly winds sweep air inland from the ocean, the steadily rising terrain drives it upwards. Once the air gets above a certain altitude, most of its moisture turns into ice crystals, and these fall as snow. As a result, the Cascade Range in winter is like a gigantic snowmaking machine, its highest peaks vying with each other for the title of snowiest place on Earth.

Measuring snowfall is not straightforward. The snow melts, and it also drifts in the wind once it has touched down

ICE AND FIRE Like many peaks in the Cascade Range, Mount Baker in Washington State is an active volcano – its last eruption was in 1880. It is also one of the world's snowiest mountains.

SNOW

on the ground. To make matters more complicated, new snow gradually compresses the older snow beneath it, squeezing out its air. Snowfall measurements are accurate only if they are taken daily, even if that means trudging out into a blizzard with a measuring stick. In spite of these difficulties, experts have recorded several world records in the Cascades. In the 12 months between February 1971 and February 1972, Mount Rainier, near Seattle in the northern part of the range, established a snowfall record of 28.5 m – roughly the height of a four-storey building. Then in 1998–99, Mount Baker, a little farther north, set a new record of 28.96 m. Mount Shasta, in northern California, holds the record for the greatest amount of snow in a single storm – in February 1959, 4.8 m of snow fell in just five days. And these figures come only from recognised weather stations. It is quite likely that some inaccessible slopes hidden away in the Cascades are snowier still.

A sheltering layer

While snowfalls like those of the Cascade Range can create problems for people, mountain animals and plants are well adapted to them. Conifers shrug snow off their sloping branches. Other plants may suffer damage from the weight of snow that is pressing down on them, but a few actually benefit – branches pushed down to the ground sometimes develop roots and so the plant spreads.

For smaller mountain plants, a covering of snow is an insulator against the winter cold, preventing the temperature of the soil dropping much below zero. Where the snow cover is less thick, a 'greenhouse effect' may even be created, allowing plants growing there to get a head start in spring. Sheltered beneath the thinner layer of snow, the plants receive enough sunlight to start photosynthesis a few weeks before the snow melts. Among animals, voles and other small rodents carry on daily life beneath the snow – for them, thick snow is a welcome shield against predators, which lasts until the spring thaw.

EARLY START Springs comes abruptly in Tibet's Kangshung Valley, as purple daisies and other mountain plants burst into bloom (below). Many of these plants start growing before the snow melts – the cover protects them from late frosts.

IN 1903, SCIENTISTS FROM THE BRITISH EXPEDITION SHIP *DISCOVERY* SET FOOT IN ANTARCTICA'S DRY VALLEYS. The team, led by Robert Falcon Scott on his first Antarctic expedition, were astonished to find themselves crunching their way across bone-dry gravel sculpted by the wind. There were no signs of life around them, apart from the mummified corpses of seals that had got lost and died there many centuries ago.

With their bare rock and bizarre climate, Antarctica's Dry Valleys have fascinated researchers ever since. They lie close to McMurdo Sound, an ice-filled inlet of the Ross Sea, and together cover a total area of about 4000 km² – roughly 2 per cent of Antarctica as a whole. Even from high up, their dark sandstone rock, almost devoid of ice, makes them look totally different from the inland ice sheet and the glaciers that connect the ice sheet with the sea.

High dry winds

Antarctica owes its present shape to a geological upheaval more than 45 million years ago, which created the Transantarctic Mountains, stretching across the continent, and the Dry Valleys, which run at right angles from the mountains towards the sea. Initially, the valleys were filled with ice, but later the ice retreated, revealing bare rock. Rock absorbs heat from sunshine, which has helped to keep the valleys largely free of ice, but a more important factor is fierce katabatic winds – winds driven by gravity, blowing when cold dense air sinks under its own weight. The Antarctic ice sheet creates the coldest air on the Earth's surface, and this gathers speed as it sinks towards

DRY COLD

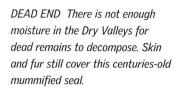

DEAD END There is not enough moisture in the Dry Valleys for dead remains to decompose. Skin and fur still cover this centuries-old mummified seal.

the coast. By the time it reaches the Dry Valleys, it whistles down them at more than 300 km/h, clearing away fallen snow and evaporating pockets of ice.

Some of the Dry Valleys have liquid water, contained in highly saline lakes, up to 5 km long. A few are frozen solid all year round, but others contain liquid water under a thick covering of permanent ice. The largest, Lake Vanda, is fed by the Onyx River, which gets its water from a tongue of glacial ice 30 km away. For a few weeks each summer, the Onyx is Antarctica's longest river, until temperatures drop again and its flow comes to a halt.

Valley micro-life

In 1903, *Discovery*'s scientists concluded that the Dry Valleys were devoid of life. It is true that there are no birds, insects or plants, or even traces of the lichens that grow on bare rocks near Antarctica's shores, but the valleys do have micro-organisms. Some of these live just under the surface of rocks, where pores and cracks protect them from the deadly katabatic winds. The majority are bacteria and algae, which live by harnessing the energy in sunlight in the same way as plants. For six months each year, they grow and reproduce in the non-stop daylight of the Antarctic summer, collecting tiny amounts of moisture before it evaporates in the wind. For the remaining six months, the microbes shut down, and wait until the Sun rises once more. When they die, they provide food for equally tiny fungi, creating some of Earth's smallest and simplest communities of living things.

Microbes have also been found in the lakes. Lake Vanda has the richest collection because of its ice cover. During the summer, this acts like a one-way lens, collecting heat and transmitting it to the water below. Near the bottom, where the water is saltiest, the temperature reaches 23°C. This warmth supports bacteria, fungi and yeasts. In 2002, scientists drilling into the lake's ice covering found microbes that had been frozen for nearly 3000 years. When thawed out, they came to life.

PATTERNED GROUND Sandstone cliffs rise on either side of Farnell Valley, one of Antarctica's Dry Valleys. Cycles of freezing and thawing over hundreds of years have created polygonal gaps in the gravel on the valley floor, revealing the underlying ground ice.

THE BIG
THAW

IN THE FAR NORTH, THE SPRING THAW IS THE BIGGEST EVENT IN THE CALENDAR. In the space of a few weeks, the entire Arctic landscape changes, making life easier for most animals, but creating problems for others that exploit the winter ice. The thaw is good news for millions of migrating birds that arrive on the treeless tundra to breed, often before the snow has completely disappeared, but it is a lot less welcome for the Arctic's largest predator, the polar bear. As the sea ice shrinks in spring, polar bears swap life on the frozen ocean for a largely land-based one. With this comes a change of diet – from seals to much smaller animals and even berries and shoots. By the time autumn arrives and the sea ice starts to re-form, many polar bears have lost up to a third of their body weight.

Other hunters that fare better in winter are wolverines, large members of the weasel family, which are much faster on a frozen surface than on soft, ice-free ground. In winter, their prey may include animals as big as moose. During the summer, they have to get more of their food by climbing trees, where they raid the nests of birds or squirrels, or by scavenging for dead remains.

According to an old Russian tradition, spring is not a time to go on long journeys. It is easy to see why. As the thaw sets in, unpaved roads turn into muddy slurry and vehicles can get bogged down for days on end.

Pingos and polygons

In the High Arctic – which includes the most barren, northerly Arctic regions – the annual cycle of freezing and thawing affects the landscape in other ways, too. In some places, blocks of frozen

ADAPTABLE CAT *An American cougar (also called puma or mountain lion) stands on the ice of a partially frozen river. Cougars can thrive in a wide range of habitats, from Arctic tundra in the Canadian Yukon to tropical rain forest.*

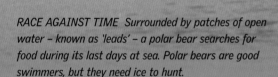

RACE AGAINST TIME *Surrounded by patches of open water – known as 'leads' – a polar bear searches for food during its last days at sea. Polar bears are good swimmers, but they need ice to hunt.*

groundwater form under the surface, pushing up the soil above them to produce mounds, called 'pingos'. These look like miniature volcanoes, up to 70 m high.

Elsewhere, piles of stones are stretched out in striking geometric patterns, called polygons, which make the surface of the ground look like an enormous honeycomb. It is not known exactly how the polygons form, but scientists at the University of California, Santa Cruz, believe that they may result from an interaction of two processes. In one process, the cycle of freeze and thaw and the formation of blocks of frozen groundwater force the soil upwards in some areas. Over time, stones will move towards the edges of the 'upwelling' area, naturally sorting themselves out from the finer-grained material in the soil. This leaves a zone of fine-grained soil surrounded by a rim of stones. The second process is the result of further freezing and thawing, during which the stones are squeezed and lengthened into geometric shapes.

ICE CLASSIC: A LOTTERY ON ICE

Every year in Alaska, thousands of dollars are raised for charity in one of the world's most unusual lotteries. People taking part have to guess the exact moment when the frozen Tanana River will start its spring break-up. The tradition dates to 1917, when engineers wanting to monitor the break-up erected a wooden tripod on the river – when it toppled, they knew that the break-up had begun. Since then, the Ice Classic has become an Alaskan tradition and a source of valuable data on climate change. The earliest break-ups occurred on April 20 in 1940 and 1998. The latest, May 20, followed an exceptionally cold winter in 1963–64.

HIGHS
LOWS

AND 4

THE EARLY MORNING LIGHT PICKS OUT
THE SHEER ROCK WALLS OF CERRO TORRE,
one of a group of towering rock pinnacles
and spires in southern Patagonia. Every
continent has isolated high spots like these –
massive mountain peaks where the weather
is often violent and the temperature below
freezing. Because of their height, even
mountains near the Equator are covered with
snow and ice at their summit. And it is not
just in mountain ranges that dizzying heights
occur. Rivers cut down through plateaux to
form deep canyons, waves and storms carve
out sea cliffs, and frosts sheer off great slabs
from vertical rock faces. At the other
extreme, the continents' lowest points are all
in desert regions where the Sun burns away
all moisture. In deserts, as in mountains, only
the hardiest life forms survive.

ULTRA MOUNTAINS

SOME OF THE WORLD'S REMOTEST REGIONS ARE HOME TO MEMBERS OF AN EXCLUSIVE CLUB – mountain peaks that stand proud against the skyline, reigning supreme over their surroundings. While many of the world's highest mountains have multiple peaks, or close neighbours that rival them in altitude, the isolation of ultra-prominent peaks, or ultras, gives them an awe-inspiring majesty that can be out of all proportion to their height. Throughout history, ultras have been recognised as something special. One of the best-known, Japan's Mount Fuji, has been a recurring image for centuries in paintings and poetry. Like all ultras it has an aura of lofty isolation, and at 3776 m its snow-capped peak often projects above the clouds.

Some of the world's most famous and spectacular peaks are not on the list of ultras. Neither the Matterhorn nor the Eiger – classic climbs in the European Alps – qualify. This is because ultras are not just big and bold: they have to fulfil another criterion as well.

SOLITARY SPLENDOUR Mount Chimborazo, in the Ecuadorian Andes, has a prominence of 4122 m. Its glacier-covered summit is the most distant point from the Earth's centre.

Measuring up to prominence

To understand what makes an ultra, imagine a mountain standing in rugged terrain. Next, imagine that the sea is rising so that it starts to overrun the lower ground. As the water level creeps upwards, more and more hilltops become islands, then start to disappear. The water continues rising and laps at the mountain's sides. Eventually, a critical point is reached: the mountain becomes an island, cut off from all the high ground around it. When this happens, imagine stopping the water and measuring the island's height above the surface. This is the mountain's prominence – the key benchmark used for distinguishing ultras.

Ultras are defined as having a prominence of at least 1500 m. For isolated volcanoes this is an easy test to pass. Mount Fuji has a prominence that exactly matches its height because its graceful slopes rise from sea level, and there is no other high ground anywhere near it. Mount Kilimanjaro in Africa, Mount Rainier in North America and Mount Cook in New Zealand are also ultras. Like Mount Fuji, they are ancient volcanoes. For mountains

SOLO SENTINEL Mount Tahat in the middle of the Sahara has a prominence of 2328 m, easily making the grade as an ultra.

that are part of ranges, the test is tougher because neighbouring summits are often connected by high ridges. K2 – one of the highest peaks in the world – has an altitude of 8611 m, but ridges to sister peaks slash its prominence to less than half this. Pikes Peak in the Rocky Mountains is 4301 m high, but its prominence is only just enough for it to scrape onto the list. Some well-known mountains fare even worse. In Europe, the Matterhorn fails despite being one of the most iconic mountains in the world.

Ultras are not always breathtakingly high. For example, the Hoggar Range in Algeria, in the centre of the Sahara, has an ultra – Mount Tahat. Its altitude is only 2908 m, but what the mountain lacks in height it makes up for in prominence, looking like a colossal boulder enveloped by the dry desert air.

In search of unnamed peaks

For mountain enthusiasts, ultras have an irresistible appeal. Their isolated summits are often hard to climb, which adds to their attraction. For several decades, cartographers and climbers have worked together to identify ultras. The current total stands at just over 1500 – a tiny fraction of the world's great mountain peaks. China has the most, followed by Canada and the USA. The greatest concentration is found in mountain ranges that have been deeply gouged by glaciers, creating isolated, jagged peaks. By contrast, high-altitude plateaux – for example in South America – have relatively few.

For every clear-cut ultra like Mount Fuji, there are dozens of potential ultras, some of which do not even have names yet. Each one has to be carefully measured from its peak downwards to find out whether it makes it onto the ultra list.

LOCKED IN ICE Antarctica's Sentinel Range presents climbers with some of the remotest and most inhospitable mountains in the world. Although not the highest peaks in the range, Mount Strybing, in the foreground, and Mount Allen, on the left, remain unclimbed.

WHEN EVEREST WAS FIRST CLIMBED, IN 1953, it seemed that, with no significant challenges left, the golden era of mountaineering had ended. But more than half a century later, some of the world's highest and most inaccessible peaks remain unclimbed. They are scattered across the globe, but three regions have more than their share: Central Asia and the two poles – the last frontiers of modern climbing.

No one knows how many major peaks remain to be climbed in the Himalayan chain, partly because the peaks themselves are hard to define. For nearly 50 years after the conquest of Everest, 8414 m Lhotse Middle, or East – Everest's neighbour on the Tibet/Nepal border – was the highest. Lhotse is a huge mountain with a south face that is the steepest of its size in the world, but it has three peaks – the main summit, Lhotse Middle and Lhotse Shar. Because the Middle peak is closely connected to the 8516 m main summit, which was climbed in 1956, some mountaineers maintain that Lhotse Middle is a subsidiary peak rather than a separate mountain. Lhotse Shar was climbed in 1979, and when a Russian expedition finally conquered Lhotse Middle in 2001, the disagreement was finally put aside: the entire mountain – or all three of them – had been climbed.

By an odd quirk of statistics, the 8000 m level marks an important cut-off point in the Himalayas. Above this are the elite among the world's highest mountains –

CHALLENGING PEAKS

between 14 and 17 peaks, depending on how they are defined. All these peaks have been successfully scaled, some of them many times, but between 7000 m and 8000 m, dozens of Himalayan summits have yet to feel the imprint of a single climber's boot.

There is no dispute about the current highest unclimbed peak. It is Gangkhar Puensum, which straddles the border between Bhutan and Tibet. It has an altitude of 7570 m and is ranked the 40th-highest mountain in the world. Several attempts on the summit were made during the 1980s, but none met with success. At this point, problems of a different kind set in. To the Bhutanese, mountains are sacred places, to be revered rather than climbed. In 1994 the Bhutan government imposed a mountaineering ban on peaks over 6000 m, and in 2003 they banned all climbing. Gangkhar Puensum is likely to remain at the top of the unclimbed list for many years to come.

Counting down from Gangkhar Puensum, the Himalayas include all five highest unclimbed peaks over 7000 m. North America has many unclimbed peaks below 4000 m, particularly in remote regions such as Alaska's Arctic National Wildlife Refuge. In Central and South America, the figure is less easy to gauge. The Incas are known to have climbed several peaks in the Andes, including the world's second-highest volcano, Llullaillaco, which is 6739 m high. It is even possible that native South Americans climbed Aconcagua, the highest peak on the continent, although no firm evidence of this has been found. Fittingly perhaps, the home of modern mountaineering – Europe – has no unclimbed peaks at all.

Polar mountaineering

Accessibility, or lack of it, is a key factor in mountaineering. At nearly 5000 m, Mont Blanc is the highest mountain in western Europe, but it is relatively easy to climb, and getting to it could not be easier, with roads and even a railway line just a few

The Arctic's highest mountain, Gunnbjørn Fjeld, is an island of rock surrounded by a sea of glacial ice. Just getting to it is a major undertaking as supplies and equipment have to be transported on skis.

kilometres away. In stark contrast, polar mountains are a much greater challenge. The Arctic's highest mountain, Gunnbjørn Fjeld, lies inland from Greenland's east coast – itself one of the most sparsely populated places in the Northern Hemisphere. Almost 4000 m high, the mountain forms a nunatak – an island of rock surrounded by a sea of glacial ice. Just getting to it is a major undertaking as all supplies and equipment have to be transported on skis. After the journey across the ice, the climb is fairly straightforward as long as the weather holds.

Gunnbjørn Fjeld was first climbed in 1935, but many other Arctic mountains remain unexplored. At the other end of the world, the number is even greater. Antarctica is a mountainous continent. Its tallest peak – Mount Vinson – was discovered by a US navy reconnaissance plane only in 1957. Mount Vinson is in the Sentinel Range, near the Ronne Ice Shelf, surrounded by a vast frozen wilderness. The peak, which is 4897 m above sea level, was first climbed during the endless daylight of Antarctica's midsummer in December 1966.

Because it is so inaccessible and so mountainous, the Antarctic contains far more unclimbed peaks than the Arctic. It also has the world's most remote volcanoes. Mount Erebus, on Ross Island, is the southernmost active volcano on Earth. When it was discovered, by Sir James Clark Ross in 1841, a major eruption was in progress. However, compared to Mount Vinson, its coastal position makes Erebus relatively easy to get to and it was one of the first Antarctic mountains to be climbed, in 1908.

The Seven Summits

The successful ascent of Mount Vinson was an important milestone in mountaineering history as it was the last of the highest mountains on each continent to be climbed. But mountaineers have an unquenchable thirst for records, and it was not long before some started to wonder if a single climber could scale them all. It was – and still is – an extraordinary challenge taking in a wide variety of climbs. At one extreme is Australia's Mount Kosciuszko – the lowest of the seven at 2228 m and no more than a gentle walk. At the other extreme are two of the world's most dangerous climbs: Mount McKinley (Denali) in Alaska and Mount Everest. In between are the four other summits: Kilimanjaro in Africa, Aconcagua in South America, Antarctica's Mount Vinson, and Mount Elbrus – a 5642 m peak in Europe's Caucasus Range.

The first person to climb the Seven Summits was US climber Richard Bass, in 1985. Since then, about 200 climbers have followed in his footsteps, but not all have scaled the same seven peaks that he did. The great mountaineer Reinhold Messner drew up an alternative list that includes Puncak Jaya on the island of New Guinea instead of Mount Kosciuszko, on the grounds that New Guinea lies within Australasia. Puncak Jaya (also known as Mount Carstensz or Carstensz Pyramid), is 4884 m high and its upper slopes have some of the very few glaciers that lie close to the Equator. Getting to it requires a long trek through tropical forest – an extraordinary contrast to Mount Vinson with its glacial ice and windswept snow.

PROTECTED PEAK Dawn light catches the unclimbed summit of Gangkhar Puensum, in Bhutan. The closest neighbouring peak, Kanchenjunga, is over 200 km away.

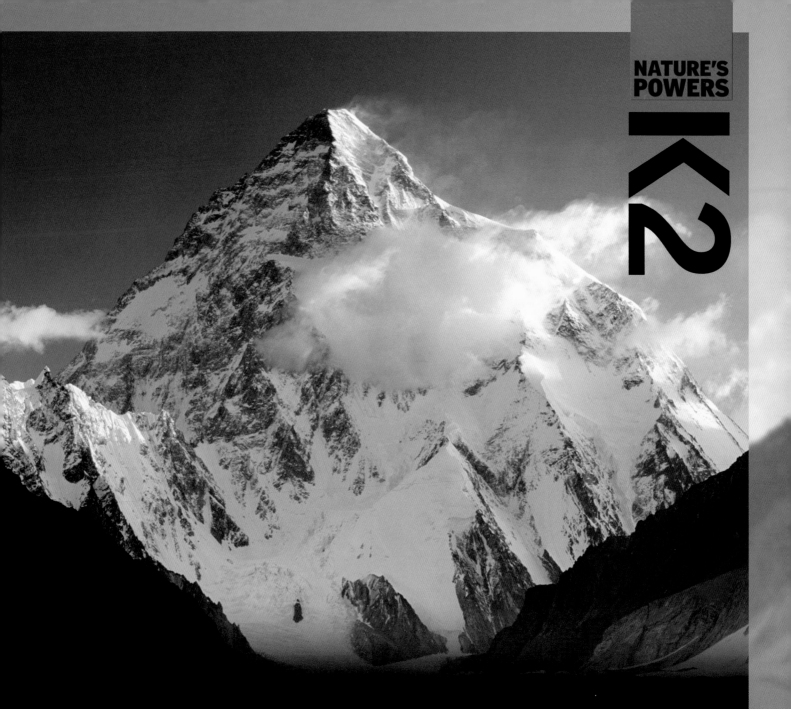

RANKED THE MOST DIFFICULT AND DANGEROUS MOUNTAIN IN THE WORLD BY CLIMBERS, K2 IS THE SECOND-HIGHEST MOUNTAIN AFTER EVEREST.

It lies in the Karakoram Range, west of the Himalayas. The Karakorams are a chain of exceptionally jagged peaks carved out by glacial ice. The range contains five peaks over 8000 m, as well as some of the world's highest cliff faces and more than a hundred major glaciers. One of these, the Baltoro Glacier, is often used by climbers to approach the K2 base camp, which lies at just over 5000 m. The first significant attempts on K2 were made in the 1930s. By 1938 the peak remained unconquered, but the altitude record had risen to about 8000 m. The final 600 m proved costly. In 1939, four climbers lost their lives; in 1953, a team of American climbers was trapped high on the mountain when one became critically ill. The sick team member died, but the outcome was almost far worse. During one section of the climb, the team had a mass fall: fortunately, a single climber managed to keep hold of the rope while the others regained their footing. This dramatic expedition was a prelude to the first successful ascent, in 1954. A team of Italian climbers reached the summit, conquering a mountain that was once thought impossible to climb. Since then fewer than 300 people have stood on K2's peak. With more than 60 fatalities, it has lived up to its reputation. In 1986 – the worst year on record – 13 climbers died.

VITAL STATISTICS

LOCAL NAME: Chogori Feng
LOCATION: Pakistan/China border
RANGE: Karakoram
ELEVATION: 8611 m (ranked 2nd)
PROMINENCE: 4017 m (ranked 22nd)
FIRST ASCENT: 1954
KEY FEATURE: The degree of
   steepness on all sides is
   unmatched in the world

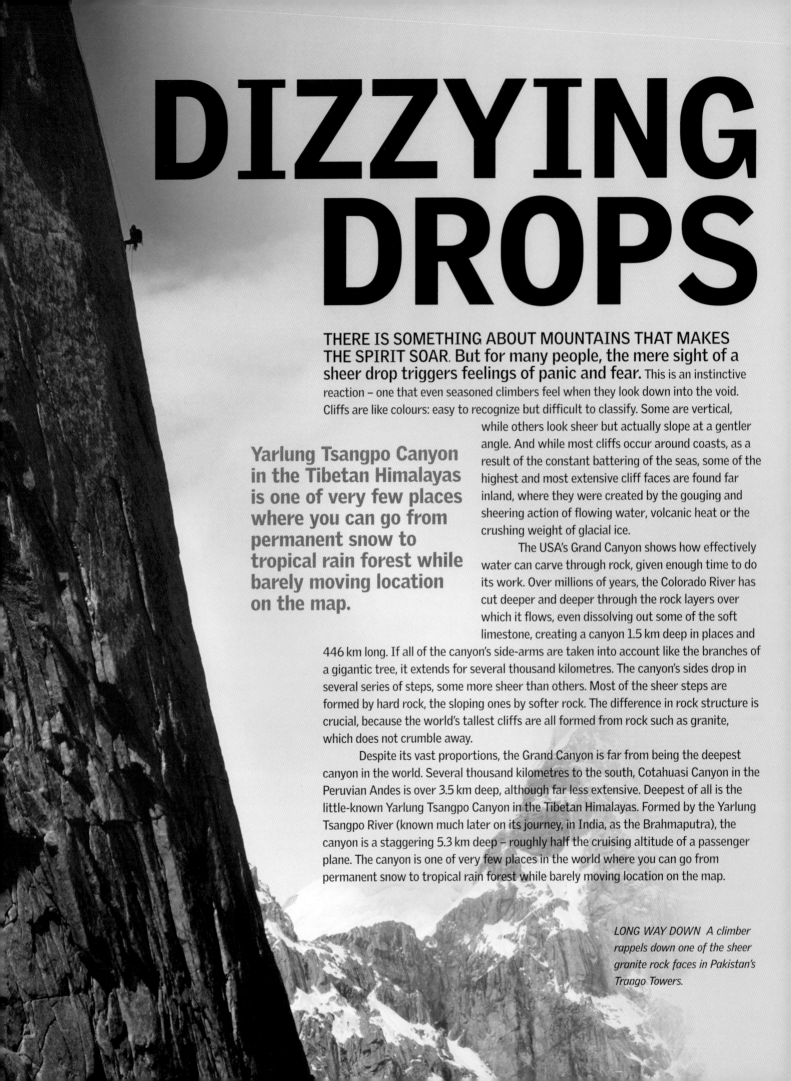

DIZZYING DROPS

THERE IS SOMETHING ABOUT MOUNTAINS THAT MAKES THE SPIRIT SOAR. But for many people, the mere sight of a sheer drop triggers feelings of panic and fear. This is an instinctive reaction – one that even seasoned climbers feel when they look down into the void. Cliffs are like colours: easy to recognize but difficult to classify. Some are vertical, while others look sheer but actually slope at a gentler angle. And while most cliffs occur around coasts, as a result of the constant battering of the seas, some of the highest and most extensive cliff faces are found far inland, where they were created by the gouging and sheering action of flowing water, volcanic heat or the crushing weight of glacial ice.

Yarlung Tsangpo Canyon in the Tibetan Himalayas is one of very few places where you can go from permanent snow to tropical rain forest while barely moving location on the map.

The USA's Grand Canyon shows how effectively water can carve through rock, given enough time to do its work. Over millions of years, the Colorado River has cut deeper and deeper through the rock layers over which it flows, even dissolving out some of the soft limestone, creating a canyon 1.5 km deep in places and 446 km long. If all of the canyon's side-arms are taken into account like the branches of a gigantic tree, it extends for several thousand kilometres. The canyon's sides drop in several series of steps, some more sheer than others. Most of the sheer steps are formed by hard rock, the sloping ones by softer rock. The difference in rock structure is crucial, because the world's tallest cliffs are all formed from rock such as granite, which does not crumble away.

Despite its vast proportions, the Grand Canyon is far from being the deepest canyon in the world. Several thousand kilometres to the south, Cotahuasi Canyon in the Peruvian Andes is over 3.5 km deep, although far less extensive. Deepest of all is the little-known Yarlung Tsangpo Canyon in the Tibetan Himalayas. Formed by the Yarlung Tsangpo River (known much later on its journey, in India, as the Brahmaputra), the canyon is a staggering 5.3 km deep – roughly half the cruising altitude of a passenger plane. The canyon is one of very few places in the world where you can go from permanent snow to tropical rain forest while barely moving location on the map.

LONG WAY DOWN A climber rappels down one of the sheer granite rock faces in Pakistan's Trango Towers.

HANG OVER As well as having one of the highest cliff faces in the world, Mount Thor on Baffin Island has the biggest overhang. When climbers abseiled down it in 2006 they needed a rope 1.5 km long.

Over the edge

Yarlung Tsangpo is a classic, V-shaped, steep-sided river gorge. Another kind of valley, called a rift, is shaped more like a cattle trough. Rifts form where volcanic heat forces apart two sections of the Earth's crust. As the two pieces separate, the ground between them drops and a flat-bottomed valley forms. The sides – known as escarpments – may be within sight of each other or hundreds of kilometres apart.

Africa's Great Rift Valley is the largest example on Earth. In places, its sheer walls crumbled long ago, making it easy to scramble down to the valley floor. In other places, they are still sharp and steep – a sign that they are geologically young and erosion has yet to set to work – and vary in height between 600 and 2700 m. For vultures and other large birds, these steep cliffs are among the few safe places to nest in a region that bristles with predators. The birds return at dusk, setting off again at dawn when the cliffs are warmed by the rising sun.

Altogether, the Great Rift Valley is 6000 km long. Its central section in Tanzania, Kenya and Ethiopia passes through terrain where the earliest humans first evolved. In remote parts of the rift, it is still possible to imagine the world as it might have been when they were alive, more than 2 million years ago.

Climbing the Trango Towers

Although rift valleys are spectacular, they are also few and far between. The majority of the world's steepest rock faces have been carved out by glacial ice. And when glaciers retreat, frost sets to work, fracturing rocks along lines of weakness and breaking off pieces, which plunge downhill and pile up on scree slopes far below. Repeated over thousands of years, the result is classic alpine scenery. Most alpine peaks look like teeth, but in some parts of the world ice has produced mountains that look like soaring spires and towers, such as the Torres del Paine in southern Chile, the Cerro Torre in Patagonia and, tallest of all, the Trango Towers in Pakistan. The Trango Towers are not well known outside the climbing fraternity, but their vertical walls make them the skyscrapers of the alpine world.

The Trango Towers are in a remote location in Pakistan's section of the Karakoram Range. Made of granite, they are surrounded by several taller peaks, but their sheer expanse of vertical rock is unmatched. The highest of the group is Great Trango Tower, which is approximately 6285 m above sea level. Its east face is 1340 m high, which makes it the tallest vertical slab of rock in the world. The east face of Great Trango Tower has been climbed, but the two Norwegian climbers who first achieved the summit – in 1984 – lost their lives on the descent.

The world's greatest overhang

For anyone afraid of heights, there is only one thing worse than a vertical drop, and that is an overhang. Many sea cliffs overhang, provoking gut-wrenching fear in climbers and cliff-top walkers. The world's tallest overhang is not found by the sea, but inland. Mount Thor, on Baffin Island in the Canadian Arctic, rises from the tundra like a giant fang.

Mount Thor's eastern slope is rounded and makes a fairly easy climb, but the western slope is a different matter. After rocky scree near ground level, the rock face rears upwards and then outwards, forming an overhanging cliff 1250 m high. The

FACTS

THE 'TROLL WALL' IS EUROPE'S TALLEST BIG ROCK FACE

It is part of the Trolltindene Massif near Norway's west coast. Also known as the Vertical Mile, it is 1100 m high, with an overhang of 50 m at its peak. The gneiss rock face is covered with ice-filled cracks and topped by a row of jagged spires.

ON A HARDNESS scale of 0–10, the chalk in cliffs ranks about 3, while most kinds of granite measure about 7.

NORMANDY'S CHALK CLIFFS HAVE RETREATED

by between 10 and 50 cm a year in the past half century.

FACTS

overhang is about 15° from the vertical, and the top of the mountain leans out by more than 200 m measured from its base.

Mount Thor was first scaled in 1953, but the awe-inspiring west face was not climbed until 1985, an extraordinary feat that followed many unsuccessful attempts. In 2006 the cliff was the setting for the world's longest rope-descent, or abseil – something that looks easy, but can be more dangerous than climbing itself. Normally, climbers use their feet to 'bounce' down a cliff when abseiling, but because Mount Thor has such a big overhang, the entire descent had to be done dangling in mid-air.

Sea cliffs

Towering sea cliffs include world-famous beauty spots and places with dangerous reputations. Chalk cliffs are among the most striking: as well as being white, they are often sheer because as the base is undermined by the sea the cliff face above it collapses soon after. The relentless action of the waves wears away softer rock to create fissures and caves. Where caves are formed back to back, they may eventually unite, forming an arch. If the cave roof collapses, sea stacks and pinnacles are left. Some of the best examples of natural arches and pinnacles, at Étretat on the Normandy coast in France, have been a favourite subject with artists for over 150 years. The chalk layer seen at Étretat re-emerges on the opposite side of the English Channel to form the famous White Cliffs of Dover and the landmark known as Beachy Head. The highest chalk cliff in Britain, Beachy Head has an almost sheer face that drops 160 m to the sea.

The west coast of Europe abounds in sea cliffs that face the full force of Atlantic breakers. These cliffs – and others like them – are made of layered rock that develops crevices and ledges when it is attacked by waves and rain during winter storms. The crevices create living space for plants, while birds use the ledges for nesting. Some cliff-nesters breed 50 m or more up the cliff face, on ledges not much wider than a playing card. It looks hazardous, but sharp claws and a superb sense of balance prevent them falling off.

Some cliff-nesters keep to themselves, but many form breeding colonies that can be tens of thousands of birds strong. In times gone by, these colonies were an important source of human food. On lonely St Kilda, off the west coast of Scotland, eggs and young birds were collected by men lowered on home-made ropes down the cliffs, which in places are more than 250 m high.

Europe's highest sea cliffs, on the Faroe Islands, tower 750 m above the cold waters of the North Atlantic, but the tallest in the world are much higher. The title of world's highest sea cliffs goes to the north-east coast of Molokai, in the Hawaiian Islands. Molokai's cliffs are 1010 m high, the remnants of a volcano that has partially collapsed into the sea. The cliffs face the prevailing wind, which makes them one of the wettest spots on Earth, with over 5000 mm of rain a year. The rain gouges out deep gulleys in the crumbling rock, but it also supports an unbroken blanket of lush subtropical plants. These cling to every surface, from the steepest slopes near the top of the cliffs to the gentlest near the sea. The effect is like a section of tropical rain forest tipped on its side.

LIMITED SPAN At Étretat, in northern France, the sea has carved spectacular arches out of the retreating cliffs.

CARVED BY WATER The deep canyons in the cliffs of Kauai, like those on other Hawaiian Islands, have been carved by the rain.

LOST WORLDS

SEEN FROM THE AIR, THE TEPUÍS OF VENEZUELA LOOK LIKE GIANT SHIPS AFLOAT IN A SEA OF CLOUDS. **The tops of these massive sandstone outcrops are cut off from the rain forest beneath by sides of sheer rock, and even today some of them have never been climbed.** Flat-topped mountains, or mesas, are usually found in deserts, not rain forests – one reason why tepuís are so special. Another is their age. The sandstone here formed about 1.8 billion years ago, putting it among some of the oldest rocks on Earth. It was already ancient when the world's first animals appeared.

At first the rock formed a continuous layer, but about 180 million years ago it was forced upwards, creating a huge plateau. Rain then set to work, eroding the sandstone into isolated fragments, the tepuís. The largest – Auyan Tepuí – is almost 3000 m high and has a surface area half the size of New York City. Mount Roraima is almost as big, although not quite so high. A flotilla of smaller tepuís erupts from the forest. Venezuela's tepuí country – known as La Gran Sabana – has the

TALLEST TEPUÍ Cut off from the forest below by its sheer sandstone walls, immense Mount Roraima is about 2800 m above sea level.

feel of a remote frontier. Access to the foot of some of the largest tepuís requires a hike of several days through the forest. The ascent involves difficult climbing up steep gulleys that can flood within minutes of rainfall – and this is just the prelude. Sheer cliffs rise to the summit, creating some of the strangest vistas on Earth.

Although tepuís look flat-topped from a distance, they are very different at close quarters. Their surfaces are covered with blocks of sandstone, some smaller than a football, others higher than a house. Over the millennia, water has eroded these blocks into all kinds of improbable shapes resembling sculptures or curious creatures on spindly sandstone legs. Unlike the cliffs, this sandstone is almost black, making the bizarre scenery seem even more unreal. Being so high up, the tops of the tepuís are much cooler than the forest below. Even

Wherever there are plants, there are animals that eat them, and other animals that eat the plant-eaters. Tepuís are no exception, but because the plants are so small, their food webs are also on a tiny scale. The biggest plant-eaters include bugs and beetles, while on some tepuís, frogs are the largest predators. But because tepuís are isolated, and have been for millions of years, their plants and animals have evolved in different ways to those on the forest floor. As a result, many species found on the tepuís today are quite unique; Mount Roraima's marsh pitcher and black frog, for example, are found there and nowhere else.

Myth and fiction

For Venezuela's Pemón Indians, tepuís have always been sacred sites. Some myths and legends feature places on the tops of tepuís – evidence that the Pemón climbed them long ago. The first scientific expedition to a tepuí took place in the 1880s, when the botanist Everard im Thurn climbed Mount Roraima and brought a collection of plant specimens back to Europe. His lectures inspired Sir Arthur Conan Doyle, whose novel *The Lost World* was set on a tepui. Conan Doyle created a place inhabited by dinosaurs, pterodactyls and early humans rather than bromeliads and frogs.

Since then, researchers have continued to explore these lost worlds, cataloguing their plants and animals. Although they have no dinosaurs, tepuís have something else that is almost as special: they have never been settled or transformed by humans and are therefore among the ultimate wild places of the world.

though the Equator is only about 500 km away, night-time temperatures can drop as low as 5°C. During the rainy season, intense thunderstorms break out almost every day, and on the surface of a tepuí, water seems to be everywhere, searching for a route to drain away.

On some tepuís, rainwater gathers into streams and rivers before being swallowed by sinkholes, which are connected to cave systems deep within the rock. After flowing underground, the water bursts out of the tepuí hundreds of metres lower down. In most places, water takes a more direct route, rushing towards the edge of the plateau, then plunging over the cliff. Many of these waterfalls are over 250 m high, but Angel Falls, on Auyan Tepuí, holds the world's waterfall height record, tumbling more than 950 m before the water eventually hits the ground as spray.

At home in the sky

Compared to the rain forest around them, tepuís are difficult habitats for wildlife. The first problem is that there is very little soil. There are scattered pockets of soil trapped by rocks, but elsewhere it is soon washed away. Where soil does build up, it is cold and wet – unsuitable for most plants to grow in. As a result, there are no forests aboard these islands in the sky; instead, vegetation consists of low-growing plants tucked away in more favourable spots in an otherwise hostile world.

Because many lichens and mosses can survive on bare rock surfaces, they are the commonest species. Among flowering plants, some of the most successful are spiky-leaved bromeliads, often no more than ankle-high. But the real specialists at this high life are carnivores, such as pitcher plants and sundews. By catching and digesting insects, these plants get some of the nutrients that most other plants collect from soil.

UNDERCOVER ANTS This slender-bodied ant is found only on tepuís, where it searches the rocks for food.

THERE ARE PLACES IN THE WORLD WHERE IT IS POSSIBLE TO VENTURE HUNDREDS OF METRES BELOW SEA LEVEL BUT NOT GET WET. These natural depressions include some of the harshest and hottest places on Earth, as well as remote oases thousands of kilometres from the sea. The world's deepest depression is the valley of the River Jordan, which runs parallel to the Mediterranean's eastern shore. Instead of flowing to the coast, the Jordan ends in an inland lake – the Dead Sea. At 420 m below sea level, the Dead Sea's shoreline is the lowest point anywhere on dry land apart from caves and man-made mines. Gravity is stronger here than at other points on the Earth's surface, the air is more dense, and, because the Dead Sea is nearly nine times more saline than the oceans, the water moves sluggishly. With so much dissolved salt, the lake is off-limits to almost all forms of life apart from the toughest bacteria. The water buoys up swimmers like corks and leaves crunchy crystals wherever waves break along the shore.

The Dead Sea has a strangely closed-in feel. As well as being biologically barren, it is also a dead end for the River Jordan. Water flows into the depression, but it

LOW POINT Salt-encrusted mud surrounds the spring at Badwater Basin, the lowest point in North America. The water quickly evaporates, leaving crystals of salt and other minerals.

ULTRA LOWS

DEEP HEAT Hot, mineral-laden springs erupting from the ground in the Danakil Depression create colourful formations.

cannot flow out. Instead, it evaporates into the bone-dry desert air. This is a characteristic of depressions: instead of filling up with water, they shed it as fast as they collect it – sometimes faster.

America's deepest point

North America's deepest depression is Badwater Basin in the central section of Death Valley. At this aptly named spot, a small spring brings saline water to the surface 86 m below sea level. Most of the time the spring is surrounded by a cracked crust of salty mud. It is not a place to linger: north of here is Furnace Creek, one of the hottest places in the world. For most animals, the combination of heat and salt is unwelcome. Any birds that touch down here soon move on. Yet Badwater Basin is home to water plants and a freshwater snail.

Death Valley is not the deepest depression in the Americas. That title goes to the Laguna del Carbón, a salt lake in Argentinian Patagonia. Although only a few dozen kilometres from the Atlantic coast, the lake is 105 m below sea level. Today, this windswept part of South America is a largely treeless landscape used for farming sheep, but fossils reveal a very different past. Dinosaur bones have been found near the lake's shores, and petrified treetrunks show that the area was once covered by forest that stretched to the Andes more than 300 km away.

The 'most hellish place on Earth'

If the sea suddenly flooded all the world's depressions, North and South America would escape relatively unchanged. But elsewhere in the world there would be far-reaching alterations

to the map. In the Horn of Africa, the Danakil Depression would disappear underwater – something that geologists expect to happen within the next 50 million years.

The Danakil Depression has been described as the most hellish place on Earth. Set in a northern fork of Africa's Great Rift Valley, it runs parallel to the Red Sea through Djibouti, Ethiopia and Eritrea. Close by is the lowest point in Africa – the shore of Lake Asal, at 155 m below sea level. The Danakil Depression is Africa's hottest place, with temperatures reaching 40°C or more all year. Some of the Earth's lowest volcanic craters are here, and the ground is peppered with springs of hot, acidic water and steaming vents. The entire region is prone to earthquakes and volcanic eruptions triggered by widening faults in the Earth's crust. Long ago it was the habitat of humanity's ancestors, but today it produces just one useful commodity, salt, which is extracted by the local Afar people using centuries-old methods. Unlike some minerals, salt is in little danger of running out: in places the deposits are hundreds of metres deep.

Depressions in Asia

The world's most landlocked depression is in Asia, in the Chinese province of Xinjiang, surrounded by mountains and desert. It forms an oasis close to the ancient Silk Road that once connected China and the West. This remote outpost is dwarfed by Asia's largest depression – a vast area of low-lying land around the northern shore of the Caspian Sea. The Caspian is the world's biggest lake, and by far the biggest without an outlet. Its surface is 28 m below true sea level, and nearly all of its water comes from the mighty Volga – the river that drains most of western Russia. If the Caspian was connected to the oceans, parts of its northern shore would flood, inundating an area almost the size of Texas.

FACTS
LAKE EYRE IS AUSTRALIA'S LOWEST POINT, 15 M BELOW
sea level. Located in the continent's arid heart, the lake is fed by a massive river basin, but it contains water only after heavy rain – about once every three or four years. At other times, the surface is encrusted with salt. When the lake does fill, millions of water birds fly in to take advantage.

CREATED BY ACCIDENT
during canal works in 1905, the Salton Sea is a 1000 km² lake in California's Salton Sink depression.

LAKE ASAL
IS THE SALTIEST
lake on Earth, with water nearly 12 times as saline as the sea.

FACTS

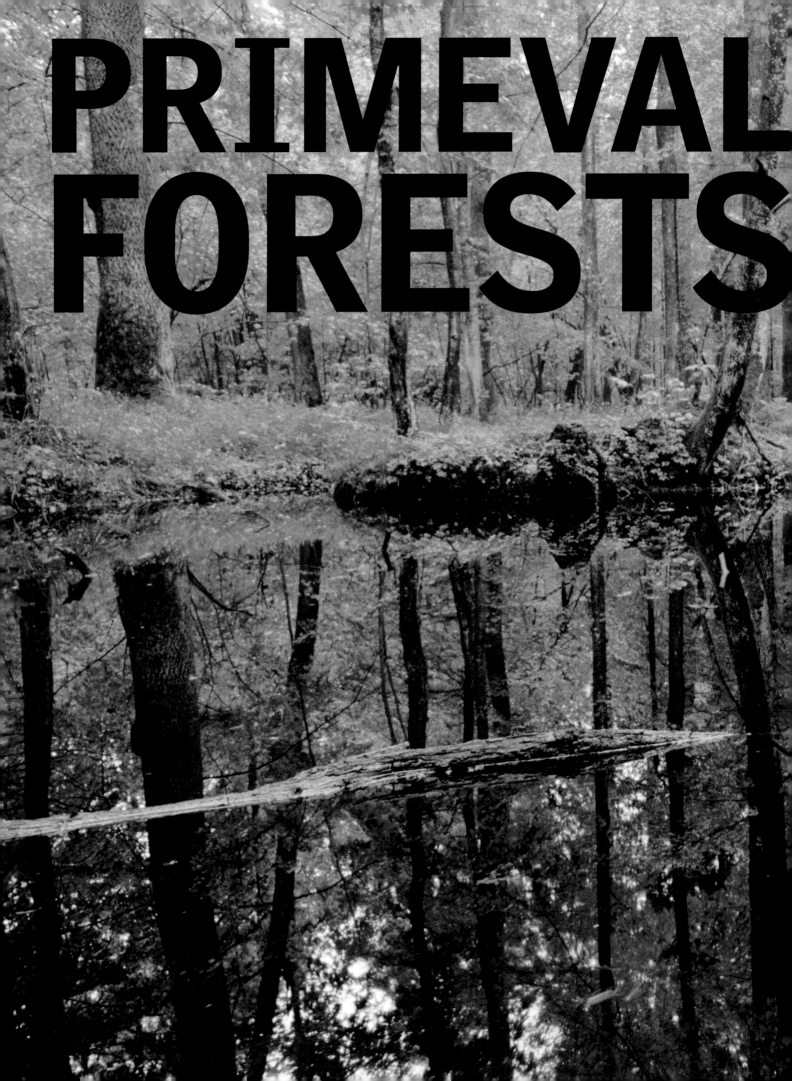

PRIMEVAL FORESTS

5

STEPPING INTO THE ANCIENT FOREST OF BIALOWIEZA (LEFT), A VAST WOODLAND SHARED BY POLAND AND BELARUS, is to be transported back tens of thousands of years. At this time, a great wildwood stretched across most of Europe, and nearly a third of the Earth's surface was covered by trees. Some parts of the world were entirely hidden by continuous forest, and trees often grew to tremendous heights and ages. It was man – and the axe – who finally changed all this for better or worse. Much of the world's original forest was cleared to make way for farming and the landscape changed irrevocably. Even so, large expanses of primeval forest survive to this day. From Russia to Tierra del Fuego, they give a glimpse of a different world – one where humans are intruders, and where the forest and its animals and plants are still truly wild.

TALES FROM THE TAIGA

RUSSIA'S TAIGA IS THE GREATEST SINGLE TRACT OF FOREST ON EARTH – a vast wilderness of endless space, solitude and eerie silence.

Taiga, or boreal forest, stretches in a wide band across North America, Europe and Asia south of the tundra. Russia has by far the largest share. Here, the taiga spreads across 11 time zones, between the Baltic Sea coast in the west and the cold shores of the Bering Sea to the east. Seen from space at night, bright lights pick out isolated cities, but apart from these signs of life, the forest itself is almost entirely dark.

Despite its great size, the taiga is dominated by a remarkably small variety of trees. All of them are conifers, and most keep their leaves all year round. The Siberian spruce grows from the Urals all the way to Russia's far east, the Siberian fir from Moscow as far as the border with China, and the Scots pine is found across the whole of Russia, and in many parts of Europe as well. The hold that these trees have on the taiga is phenomenal: no other forest on Earth contains so few species, or changes so little over such incredible distances.

Spruces, firs and pines have tough evergreen leaves – something that makes them good at coping with extreme winter cold as well as summer warmth. But the taiga's toughest tree, the Dahurian larch, sheds all its needles in the autumn, and

spends the next six months or more with its branches completely bare. The Dahurian larch grows on the northernmost edge of the taiga, where the stunted forest finally gives way to the bleak rock-strewn tundra. It can survive winter temperatures as low as −70°C, making it the hardiest tree in the world. Ironically, it is a difficult tree to grow elsewhere, because a warm spring can trick it into leaf too early, leaving it at risk from frost.

Life on the forest floor

Unlike the leaves of most broadleaf trees, conifer leaves usually last for several years. When they do fall, they take a long time to break down. The result is a springy, interlocking layer of dead needles and scales – one that wood ants collect and use as a building material. They heap the leaves around a rotting stump and after several months the nest may be 2 m high. During the summer, worker ants fan out from the nest, climbing high into the treetops to hunt for caterpillars and other insects. In the winter, many of the worker ants die, but the queen ants survive in special

RETURN OF THE WOLF The Russian taiga is one of the few parts of the world where grey wolves are on the increase. This is partly due to forestry, which opens up parts of the taiga, giving the animals more room to hunt.

ON THE LOOKOUT The great grey owl's prominent facial disk channels sounds into its ears. One of the world's largest owls, the great grey hunts by listening and watching for small animals from a perch a few metres about the ground.

chambers deep in the ground. Wood ants are voracious predators, and they help to keep the forest's insect pests in check. At one time, foresters often destroyed their nests, but today they are more often protected.

Because the leaf litter contains air spaces, it works like an insulating carpet and muffles sound. Fresh snow works in the same way, But in the middle of the Russian winter, when the ground is frozen hard, animal calls, including the haunting howls of wolves, can carry for great distances. The taiga is also one of the best places in the world to hear owls, with a dozen species in the European taiga alone. Some are summer visitors, but others, like the great grey owl, live in the forest all year round.

DEEPEST APPALACHIA

THE GREAT SMOKY MOUNTAINS, IN THE EASTERN UNITED STATES, are the setting for some of the richest broadleaf forests in the northern hemisphere. Here, deep ravines known as coves are often home to dozens of different kinds of trees, along with hundreds of species of flowers.

The reason for such an abundance of flora can be traced back to momentous events in North America's deep past. On four separate occasions in the last 2 million years, immense ice sheets have spread southwards across the continent, bulldozing rocks, soil and trees. Each time, the ice has come close to the Great Smoky Mountains, but has then stopped and retreated, almost as if it had changed its mind. The effects of these glacial cycles on the ground are clear to see. Where the ice once stood,

SPRING AWAKENING White-flowered trilliums carpet an Appalachian woodland in spring. After they have flowered, the plants produce small seeds that are spread by ants.

today's forests contain relatively few plants, and most of the trees are cold-resistant conifers. But in the heart of the Great Smoky Mountains, cove forests seem to overflow with lush broadleaf trees, and with wildflowers that bloom before the leafy canopy closes overhead in spring. Winters here can be cold, but on humid days in summer, the luxuriance of the tropics can feel just a short distance away.

The Great Smoky Mountains form part of the Appalachians, an ancient range that runs the whole length of eastern North America. At one time, the entire chain was covered with forest, but this was one of the first regions to be cleared when Europeans settlers arrived and began to farm. In time, many of those farmers moved further west, and the land gradually fell into disuse. Little by little, nature reclaimed abandoned farms, trees moved back in and the hard-won fields disappeared. By the 20th century, the true value of the Smokies was beginning to be appreciated, and in the 1930s part of the forest was given protection as a new national park – the Great Smoky Mountains National Park. Here, the soaring trunks of tulip trees can reach 40 m high, while ash trees and basswoods compete for a share of the light. Alongside the many trees grows a profusion of flowering and non-flowering plants, including trilliums, azaleas and ferns.

Appalachia's amphibians

The Smokies are one of America's most popular hiking destinations, attracting millions of people each year. Despite this human influx, they remain unspoiled, and the cove forests are home to some of North America's best-known forest animals, including the black bear and white-tailed deer. In summer, they teem with insect-eating birds.

The mountain-forest environment also provides an ideal habitat for salamanders – slow-moving amphibians with stubby legs and slender tails. Many of them breed in water, although unlike other amphibians, some 'fast forward' through the early days of their lives, turning from tadpoles to miniature adults before they have even hatched. So far, over 30 species of these primeval-looking creatures have been identified in the Appalachians, together with dozens of local breeds. Some scientists think that many of these are species in their own right, pushing the total to 100 or more. Among amphibians, this kind of richness is unsurpassed, even in the tropics, and it has earned the southern Appalachians the nickname of 'salamander capital of the world'.

TOXIC CARPET The shiny leaves of May apples cover the ground in spring (above). All parts of the plant are toxic, apart from the greenish yellow fruit, which appears in summer.

AT THE WATER'S EDGE The northern two-lined salamander lives close to running water, and clambers into it if alarmed. Its tadpoles grow up in swamps and streams.

FORGOTTEN FOREST

STRADDLING THE BORDER BETWEEN POLAND AND BELARUS, the forest of Bialowieza is the largest surviving remnant of the great 'wildwood' that once covered most of Europe.

Forest is the natural vegetation across most of Europe, and at one time it stretched almost unbroken from northern Scotland to the Mediterranean, and eastwards to the Caucasus. It provided people with everything they needed for survival, from fuel and shelter to food. But from about 10 000 years ago, farming began to spread into Europe from the Middle East, and instead of living inside the forest, people started to clear it so that they could raise animals and crops on open ground.

This clearance started in areas of raised ground, where the forest was thinner and easier to cut or burn. It then spread to the lowlands, where the forest could be as dense as the Amazon is today. Over many centuries, practically all of the wildwood was cut down, except for a handful of places where there was good reason to leave the forest alone. For Bialowieza this was the European bison or wisent – the largest native mammal in Europe's forests, with enough meat to feed a village for a week.

ANCIENT FOREST The forest of Bialowieza has remained largely unchanged for centuries, providing a living window into Europe's past.

Wildlife

Before the arrival of agriculture, bison roamed throughout Europe's lowland forests. Their sheer size made them an irresistible target for hunters and, by medieval times, bison were already rare. Hunting them became a mark of prestige, reserved for kings and aristocrats. Special forests were set aside for bison and other 'royal' game, and poaching these animals was a capital crime. The New Forest in the south of England, for example, was established by William the Conqueror in 1079 as a royal hunting reserve, principally for deer. Bialowieza was declared a royal forest in the 1500s, by the Polish king Sigismund I, for the protection of bison, although harsh penalties were not enough to stop the animals' decline. They continued to be hunted over the centuries, particularly during the border changes and conflicts that often ravaged this part of eastern Europe. In Poland, the last wild bison

FOREST FORAGERS Using their snouts like shovels, wild boar dig up the woodland floor in search of food. The animals, which were once found across much of Europe, have a superb sense of smell, and eat almost anything, from roots and subterranean fungi to earthworms and insect grubs.

was killed in 1917, and by the late 1920s, the species had disappeared altogether from the wild. There the story might have ended, but fortunately a few dozen animals remained alive in zoos and from this small nucleus, the species was reintroduced to Bialowieza. Today, bison literally stand head and shoulders above the forest's other animals, and much work is dedicated to protecting the forest's herds.

The heart of the forest has also become a refuge for other endangered mammals. Among them are the lynx, the European otter and the grey wolf – three predators that shrink from any kind of disturbance. At night, when many hunters are afoot, the silence is broken by the call of eagle owls – Europe's biggest nocturnal hunting bird, with a wingspan of up to 1.8 m. The call is the classic owl double-hoot, so loud that it can be heard up to 5 km away. Other owls make very different sounds. Proclaiming its territory, the male barn owl gives a two-second shriek, while tawny owls perform in duets, the male hooting and the female replying with a sharp *kee-wick*. Owls are nervous performers, and they stop instantly if there is the slightest sound from the forest floor.

MATING DISPLAY With its tail fanned, a male capercaillie broadcasts its bizarre courtship call. Capercaillies spend a lot of time feeding on the ground, but roost in trees at night. Hens nest in dense cover on the ground and spend the night with their chicks until they can fly.

During the day, the most bizarre natural sounds resonating through the forest are the courtship 'songs' of the capercaillie – the largest member of the grouse family, reaching the size of a small turkey. During the breeding season in early spring, males gather at ritual sites called leks, where they strut and sing to attract passing females. Capercaillie songs have several different elements: they include clicking and wheezing noises, as well as something that sounds like the popping of a champagne cork. If a female is impressed, she allows the male to mate. If not, she watches and listens with apparent indifference, before moving on.

Stately trees

Bialowieza has dozens of ancient trees, including a number of named oaks, including Great Mamamuszi, which is the thickest oak in the forest, Emperor of the South and Southern Cross. Some of the forest's trees are in rude health, while others are beset by fungi that are eating them away from inside. When they eventually die, as the Dominator Oak did in 1992, they remain where they are – no one comes to clear their wood away.

Far from being a disaster, the death of an ancient tree brings all kinds of hidden benefits to forest wildlife. It gives young trees a bigger share of the light, and it also creates a dead-wood habitat that is lacking in most managed woodlands. The result is a forest full of variety and opportunities – the closest thing on land to the richness of a coral reef.

EUROPEAN BISON

WITH A WEIGHT OF UP TO 1 TONNE FOR FULL-GROWN MALES, THE EUROPEAN BISON – OR WISENT – IS THE HEAVIEST LAND MAMMAL ON THE EUROPEAN MAINLAND. The bison are closely related to North American bison or buffalo, but instead of living in open grassland, they are animals of broadleaf forests. They were once found in woodland throughout Europe, where they roamed in small herds of up to 30 animals, feeding on grass and leaves in summer, and acorns and twigs during the winter months. Both males and females have horns and a pronounced hump at the shoulders. The bison's impression of strength is not an illusion: females guard their young fiercely and can kill if they charge.

European bison declined over many centuries, due to hunting and habitat change, and the last wild bison was killed in the early 20th century. Full extinction was narrowly avoided because a handful remained in captivity, enabling herds to be re-established. Today, the largest herds, numbering several hundred animals, live in the forest of Bialowieza, with others in forests in Russia, Lithuania and the Ukraine. The total population in zoos and the wild is now about 3000.

VITAL STATISTICS

CLASS: Mammalia

ORDER: Artiodactyla

SPECIES: *Bison bonasus*

HABITAT: Broadleaf or mixed woodland

DISTRIBUTION: Isolated forests and zoos

KEY FEATURE: Europe's largest native land mammal

Working in the gorge, botanists have found less than 100 adult Wollemi pines – one of the smallest totals for any wild tree alive today.

DINOSAUR TREE It was at Colo Gorge in Wollemi National Park, Australia, that the long-lost Wollemi pine was discovered (right). The distinctive leaves are clearly identified in a fossil from the Jurassic period (left).

VALLEY OF THE DINOSAURS

IN SEPTEMBER 1994, A WARDEN IN AUSTRALIA'S WOLLEMI NATIONAL PARK stumbled upon the world's only known stand of Wollemi pines – the botanical equivalent of finding a herd of living dinosaurs. News of the discovery soon made headlines around the world, but it took several years for the true importance of the find to set in. The surviving Wollemi pines were hanging by a biological thread – one that could have snapped at any moment in the past million years. Their location, at the bottom of a sandstone gorge less than 200 km from Sydney, also came as a stunning surprise.

Rock paintings show that Aborigines had known of the Wollemi pine's hideout for several thousand years. When European settlers arrived on Australia's east coast, not a word leaked out about this patch of forest, hidden deep in the Blue Mountains. It stayed this way for two centuries – one of the continent's greatest biological secrets.

Wollemi pines are not true pines at all. They belong to a family of conifers called araucarias, which are scattered across the Southern Hemisphere. Centuries ago, many of them were wrongly labelled as pines, and since then the name has stuck. The Norfolk Island pine gets its name from its original home in the Pacific Ocean, while the Paraná pine comes from South America. The best-known member of the family is the Chile pine, or monkey puzzle. With its flat spiky leaves and umbrella-like shape, it is one of the most instantly recognisable trees in the world.

The Wollemi pine shares lots of family features, including large, scaly cones that disintegrate to shed their seeds. But unlike its relatives, it often has multiple stems, and a strong habit of forming clumps. Working in the gorge, botanists have found less than 100 adult Wollemi pines – one of the smallest totals for any wild tree alive today. Stranger still, most of these trees are genetically identical, which means that they shared an even smaller number of parents at some point in the past. In other words, the Wollemi pine has had an amazingly close brush with extinction, but miraculously it has survived.

When all the clumps are added together, the Wollemi pine 'forest' covers less than a hectare – roughly twice the size of a football pitch. Despite the publicity surrounding their discovery, the exact location of the trees is secret, and looks likely to remain

WINTER FOREST In their native habitat in the Andes, Chile pines get most of their water as snow. The lowest branches fall off as the trees age, giving them their umbrella-like shape.

so for many years to come. They have survived for millions of years, but only because they are cut off from the outside world. The tramp of visitors' feet – and the micro-organisms that they would bring – could prove fatal, a risk that no one wants to take.

Plant-hunters

Unlike the Wollemi pine, many of today's ornamental trees were originally discovered by professional plant-hunters. During the heyday of plant-hunting, in the 19th century, these intrepid explorers searched some of the world's most far-flung regions in search of new species, often risking life and limb in the pursuit. David Douglas, who gave his name to the Douglas fir, died in a pit trap in Hawaii, while Frank Kingdon-Ward survived a long list of accidents – including being impaled on a bamboo spike – during his

expeditions to the Himalayas and the Far East. But the great age of plant-hunting did not end in 1900. Some 'dinosaur plants' were tracked down much closer to the present day.

In 1944, a Chinese forester called Tsang Wang visited a remote village in the province of Sichuan. There, in the grounds of a temple, he found a large tree of a type that he had never seen before. He took some leaves, shoots and seeds from the tree, and sent them to a professor of botany at Nanjing, who in turn sent them to a colleague in Beijing. Eventually, the specimens arrived on the desk of Dr E. H. Merrill in Boston's Arnold Arboretum, one of the world's largest collections of trees and shrubs. Here, the 'temple tree' was identified as a living dawn redwood – a conifer that was thought to have become extinct millions of years ago. In 1948, an expedition set off for Sichuan to search for dawn redwoods in the wild. Several thousand were discovered – the remnants of a huge forest that once covered much of China.

Brought back to life

By a remarkable coincidence, the dawn redwood is one of two living fossils to have come from this part of the world. The maidenhair or ginkgo has unique fan-like leaves, and has changed little in over 80 million years. Unlike the redwood, it no longer grows in the wild – the last specimens probably disappeared several centuries ago. Fortunately, the ginkgo was saved from extinction by Chinese monks, for whom the tree is sacred and who have cultivated it in their temple gardens for thousands of years. The tree has proved to be remarkably good at growing in polluted air, and can now be seen in city streets all over the world.

For the dawn redwood and Wollemi pine, the future also looks bright. In just 60 years, the dawn redwood has become a common tree in parks and botanical gardens throughout the world, and the Wollemi pine looks like following in its footsteps.

GOLDEN COLOURS The ginkgo (right) turns bright yellow in autumn, before losing its leaves. Like conifers, it produces seeds, but not flowers.

UNDER THE VOLCANOES

THE VIRUNGA VOLCANOES COMBINE BREATHTAKING SCENERY WITH DANGEROUS TERRAIN. Their forested slopes shelter some of Africa's rarest animals, but they are also the haunt of poachers and armed militias fighting a long-running civil war. The volcanoes lie about 300 km east of Lake Victoria in a region of Africa where the Great Rift Valley divides into two separate arms. They are part of the western arm, known as the Albertine Rift (after Lake Albert at its northern end), which runs south through Uganda, Rwanda and the Democratic Republic of Congo.

QUENCHED FIRES Wisps of cloud hang over the water-filled crater of Mount Bisoke in the Virunga Mountains in Rwanda. Beyond it, thick cloud shrouds the summit of Mount Mikeno, across the border in the Democratic Republic of Congo. Both volcanoes are extinct.

SECRET WILDLIFE The lowland rain forests north of the Virungas have a reputation for harbouring many hidden animals, including the okapi – a well-camouflaged relative of the giraffe, first seen by scientists in 1918.

There are eight main volcanoes – of which the highest is Mount Karisimbi, at 4507 m above sea level – as well as dozens of other smaller cones. Most have been dormant for thousands of years, but two, Nyiragongo and Nyamuragira, are very much alive. Nyiragongo last erupted in 2002, pouring lava across the airport in the city of Goma, and forcing hundreds of thousands of people to move their already makeshift homes. Since then, a lava lake has been bubbling away in the volcano's crater, a sign that its activity has not yet faded away.

Islands in the sky

For plants and animals, the Virunga Mountains and their neighbouring peaks are like tropical islands, cut off by lower ground on all sides. These forested hideaways are home to several species of primate, including nearly a dozen kinds of monkey, such as the rare golden monkey and l'Hoest's monkey (an endangered species that nests high up in trees), chimpanzees and, most famously, mountain gorillas.

Seen from the air, most of the mountains are skirted by what looks like a patchwork quilt of green, made up of hundreds of thousands of tiny farms. Individually, the plots are small, but the volcanic soil is extremely fertile and in the damp equatorial climate crops grow throughout the year. Above the farms, the forest begins, starting with evergreen trees and shrubs, which give way at about 2500 m to bamboo. Dense thickets of bamboo

arch overhead, while dead leaves scrunch underfoot, giving the forest an unsettling feel. This habitat shelters some of the Virungas' last remaining Cape buffalo, which are notoriously aggressive, so it is not a good place to linger.

Above 3000 m, the bamboo forest becomes more stunted until finally it peters out, and at 3400 m a unique mountain habitat begins – the Afro-alpine zone, a world that alternates between freezing nights and brilliant days under the glare of the equatorial Sun. There are no true trees at these altitudes: instead, the scenery is dominated by giant soft-stemmed plants that have evolved for life high up. They include giant lobelias, which have a single enormous clump of spiky leaves, and giant groundsels, with shaggy forked stems that grow taller than a human.

Related to the low-growing garden weeds native to large parts of Europe and Asia, the giant groundsels thrive not just in the Virungas, but also on East Africa's other 'islands in the sky', including the Rwenzori Mountains, Mount Kenya and Mount Kilimanjaro. There are dozens of different species, many of which are found only on a single mountain and at

FORAGING PARTY Mountain gorillas can climb trees, but they spend most of their time on the ground. Here a silverback male (on the right) leads his troop across a clearing in the forest.

GORILLA

AFTER CHIMPANZEES, GORILLAS ARE OUR

CLOSEST LIVING RELATIVES. Physically, all gorillas look similar from a distance, with thickset bodies, long arms and massive jaws, which they use for chewing plants, but they form two separate species – the western gorilla and the eastern gorilla – living in different parts of tropical Africa. The mountain gorilla is a subspecies of the eastern gorilla and is found only in cool, damp conditions high up in Africa's Great Rift Valley. All gorillas are peaceable plant-eaters, attacking only as a last resort.

Eastern gorillas are darker than western ones, and mountain gorillas are darkest of all, with a coat that looks almost black. Once they have reached maturity at the age of about 12, adult males develop a silvery saddle on their backs. These 'silverbacks' can be twice as big as adult females and may weigh up to 200 kg. They are also the key to gorilla social life. Each one forms a family group or 'troop', which includes several females and their young. The silverback protects the troop and leads it during the daily search for food. Lowland gorillas feed mainly on fruit, but mountain gorillas eat a wide range of leaves and roots, ripping their food off with their hands and then chewing it slowly during rests on the forest floor.

Existence has become precarious for gorillas. They are threatened by deforestation, hunting and diseases passed on when they come into contact with humans. About 90 000 western gorillas survive and about 15 000 of the eastern species. Mountain gorillas, numbering just over 700, are the most threatened.

CLASS: Mammalia
ORDER: Primates
SPECIES: *Gorilla beringei beringei*
HABITAT: Mountain forests
DISTRIBUTION: Virunga Mountains and Bwindi Impenetrable Forest
KEY FEATURE: The only gorilla found at high altitude, with unusually long fur that insulates it from the cold

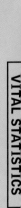

VITAL STATISTICS

THE MOST ACTIVE OF THE VIRUNGA VOLCANOES IS

Mount Nyamuragira in the Democratic Republic of Congo. It has erupted more than 25 times in the past 100 years, and one of its lava flows is more than 30 km long.

FOUNDED IN 1925, VIRUNGA NATIONAL PARK

was Africa's first national park. It covers nearly 8000 km².

GLACIERS IN THE RWENZORI

Mountains on the borders of Uganda and the Democratic Republic of Congo are among the last to survive in Africa. As the world warms, they are shrinking fast and are expected to disappear in the next 20 years.

particular altitudes. Researchers think that a single groundsel species evolved on Mount Kilimanjaro about a million years ago, and from here its floating seeds spread to smaller mountains – a case of plants leapfrogging peak to peak. Other Afro-alpine plants, such as giant lobelias, probably spread in the same way.

Gorillas in their midst

The borders of Uganda, Rwanda and the Democratic Republic of Congo meet in the Virungas, where three adjoining national parks are meant to provide protection for the region's best-known inhabitants – the mountain gorillas. Estimates vary, but there are probably fewer than 700 of these enormous vegetarians left in the wild, of which about half live in the Virungas.

Virunga National Park in the Congo has the largest number of the animals, but it also has an extremely dangerous reputation. Although bristling with armed guards, it has been infiltrated by poachers and in 2007 was the scene of two killings, which took the lives of seven gorillas, including a family patriarch or 'silverback' male. Uganda's Mgahinga Gorilla National Park is safer, but has only a small number of gorilla groups. Volcanoes National Park in Rwanda is where the US zoologist Dian Fossey founded her gorilla research centre in 1967, but it, too, has its dangers – Fossey was murdered there in 1985, a crime that has never been solved. Today, the park has several families of gorillas, which have become habituated to people, allowing visitors the unique experience of seeing the animals at first hand. This 'gorilla tourism' comes at a price – as Fossey feared it would. Habituated gorillas risk catching human diseases, and clearly the tamer they become the less they are truly wild.

RUNNING THROUGH THE TREES Most turacos live deep in Africa's forests, where they often scuttle along branches, instead of taking to the air. This attractive species is Ross's turaco, found from the Great Rift Valley westwards to Cameroon.

Impenetrable forest

North of the Virungas, Bwindi Impenetrable National Park in Uganda sounds like a map-maker's invention. In fact, this incredibly tangled jungle is one of richest ecosystems in Africa, home to a wider variety of plants than any other equivalent area in the continent, apart from the zone around the Cape of Good Hope. It has more than 200 species of trees, 100 kinds of ferns and 350 bird species.

Some of the most fascinating of the birds are the turacos and iridescent sunbirds. Turacos are heavy-bodied tree-dwellers, related to cuckoos and found only in Africa. They feed on fruit and get their sumptuous green and red colours from copper-containing chemicals that are unique in the bird world. The sunbirds, with their tiny bodies and slender, sharply pointed beaks, look very much like American hummingbirds as they speed from flower to flower, except that they perch, rather than hover, when they feed. Africa has more than 80 species of these hyperactive feathered jewels. Some are widespread; others live on individual mountains in the Great Rift Valley or on offshore islands, such as São Tomé or Socotra.

The Bwindi forest is also home to about 320 mountain gorillas, divided into two dozen or so family groups. Compared to the Virunga gorillas, the ones in Bwindi have longer legs and shorter fur and they live at lower altitudes – some zoologists think that they should be classified as a separate subspecies, more closely related to the eastern lowland gorilla in the rain forests of the Congo. The Bwindi forest has been carefully protected for many years, and its gorillas seem to be feeling the benefit. Between 2002 and 2006, park staff found that the number of gorillas had risen by about 6 per cent. Estimating numbers is a difficult task, but in a part of the world beset by misfortune, this increase is the best possible news.

IN TASMANIAN FORESTS

WESTERN TASMANIA COULD HARDLY LOOK MORE DIFFERENT FROM MAINLAND AUSTRALIA, just 250km away across the turbulent waters of the Bass Strait. The island lies in the path of the Roaring Forties, ferocious winds that swirl around the globe between latitudes 40 and 50 degrees South, capable of shedding more than 3000 mm of rain on Tasmania a year. Instead of grey-green bush shimmering in the Sun as on the mainland, the natural vegetation in Tasmania's western wilderness is temperate rain forest, spreading out beneath scudding clouds. In today's timber-hungry world the forest has become an ecological battleground, but where it has survived unscathed, trees seem to cling to every available surface, from exposed offshore islands to steep mountainsides.

Many of the forest's trees are endemic, growing nowhere else in the world, including the celery-top pine – a strangely

SPINY DEFENCE The short-beaked echidna can be remarkably tame. If it is threatened, it quickly burrows into the ground, leaving only its spines showing above the surface.

shaped tree of the higher slopes, which can survive for eight centuries or more – and the massive Huon pine, a slow-growing conifer. Tree-ring counts show that Huon pines can live for more than 2000 years. Their wood is hard, heavy and charged with scented oil, which protects it against fungal attack even after a tree has died. Unusually for a conifer, the Huon pine can form clumps – a way of reproducing without seeds. One clump in Tasmania's West Coast Range may have started life more than 10 000 years ago, when the last ice age was coming to an end.

SAVING A WILDERNESS
For most of Tasmania's history, its forests have been left virtually untouched. It has been inhabited by humans for at least 25 000 years, but felling only started in earnest in the 19th century when the island became a British penal colony with timber as one of its key products. On the west coast, Huon pine logs weighing several tonnes were cut by hand, then floated offshore at Macquarie Harbour. Later, mechanisation allowed timber companies to clear large areas of temperate rain forest, often to supply the wood-chip trade. But conservation has become a priority. In the 1980s, worldwide protests prevented the building of the proposed Franklin Dam in the heart of the rain forest. One-fifth of Tasmania has now been classified as a World Heritage Area, and many Tasmanians believe that their 'wild west' should be preserved.

Animal isolation

As ice melted across the globe and sea levels rose, Tasmania became cut off from the mainland, isolating its wildlife, except for animals that could swim or fly there. By that time, some of Australia's most fascinating animals were already aboard, including the short-beaked echidna – a roly-poly insect-eater protected by hundreds of pencil-sized spines. From a distance, it is easy to see why European settlers thought that echidnas were related to porcupines. In fact, they are egg-laying mammals or monotremes, unique to Australasia. Tasmania's echidnas are a distinct subspecies, the southernmost monotremes.

Echidnas are still common in Tasmania, and despite competition from sheep, the island's kangaroos and wombats have also survived. But two of its most famous mammals – the Tasmanian devil and the thylacine – have had very different fortunes. Originally, both lived on the Australian mainland, but the mainland animals died out, leaving Tasmania as their final stronghold.

The Tasmanian devil is the smaller of the two, a scavenger with a squat body, short legs and powerful jaws. Its bite is strong enough to crack open bones, which it swallows along with skin and teeth when it sits down to one of its lengthy meals. The difference between scavengers and

hunters is easy to misconstrue, and until the 1940s local farmers treated the Tasmanian devil as a pest. Its numbers fell sharply and today it is an endangered species, but it survives.

The thylacine, or Tasmanian tiger, was a full-time hunter and the world's biggest marsupial carnivore. When farming began in Tasmania, it was soon labelled a sheep-killer, even though no one ever established the number of sheep it actually took. Its reputation sealed its fate. The last wild thylacine was shot in 1930, and in 1933 the last known specimen died in a Tasmanian zoo, although there have been many unconfirmed sightings of thylacines in the wild since then. If the species still exists – and the likelihood is slender – it will almost certainly be somewhere in the wilderness in Tasmania's west.

FORTUNATE FEW Tasmanian devils give birth to dozens of young, but only four survive in each litter, because the females only have room for four inside their pouches. These youngsters have been weaned.

STIFLING HEAT, POISONOUS SNAKES AND THORNS THAT SNAG LIKE FISH HOOKS – all these are part of life in the Gran Chaco, a vast frontier zone of scrub and forest shared by Argentina, Bolivia, Paraguay and Brazil. Chaco is a Quechua Indian word meaning 'hunting territory', and it is not hard to see how the region earned its name. The wildlife in the Gran Chaco is rich and varied, including species that are good to hunt, such as peccaries, agoutis and pacas, and animals that most hunters would go to great lengths to avoid, including rattlesnakes and the false water cobra. Inaccessible and little visited, the region is a perfect place for anyone or anything needing to disappear.

The Gran Chaco is not just one habitat, but a succession of different ones spread out on a huge eastward-sloping plain with the great mountain chain of the Andes rising to the west. The habitats include desert, forest and emerald-green swamps, as well as seemingly endless savannah grasslands mixed with scrub and trees. The trees range from curious kapoks with bottle-shaped trunks to elegant palms, full of parrots and other fruit-eating birds. One small group of trees – the quebrachos, or 'axe-breakers' – epitomises the harsh landscape and its tendency towards extremes. With rock-hard wood and bark rich in tannins, the quebrachos were once the symbol of the Chaco, but many have been felled to make way for livestock grazing or overharvested for their tannins, used for tanning leather. As a result, the trees are now in urgent need of conservation.

The oven of South America

There are no clearly defined boundaries to the Gran Chaco, but even by conservative estimates it is immense, covering more than 600 000 km^2 – larger than France. The Tropic of Capricorn

WAX-MAKERS Huge stands of wax palms grow in areas of the Chaco that are periodically flooded. The leaves produce an exceptionally hard wax, used in polishes and lipstick.

THE GRAN CHACO

FOOT PATROL BIRD The seriema hunts on foot, catching and tearing apart its prey with sharp claws and sometimes beating it on the ground. It can fly, but only just – when confronted by danger it normally tries to run away.

divides it in two unequal parts, and one of its most noticeable features is the heat. In the heart of the Chaco, the mercury can soar above 40°C in the summer wet season, making this one of the hottest regions in South America.

At this time of year, the Chaco seems to seethe with insects, particularly after dark. Attracted by the light, enormous moths and beetles crash into outdoor lamps, while clouds of smaller insects swirl in headlight beams along the region's unmarked dirt roads. Just as in Africa, the open landscape teems with termites and ants. The Chaco is also one of the world's greatest showcases for grasshoppers, bees and wasps. Most of the bees are relatively harmless and live singly, but the wasps include some species that make nests as big as footballs and can be highly aggressive if they are disturbed.

This abundance of insect food fuels some distinctively South American animals, which evolved when the continent was still an island unconnected to North America – about 3 million years ago. Among these creatures are anteaters, armadillos and ground-feeding birds, including tinamous and seriemas. Tinamous look like game birds, such as quail or grouse, but they are not related, and feed mainly on insects and seeds. Seriemas feed on all kinds of small animals, including snakes.

The thorny Chaco scrub is good at concealing animals, particularly when they need to make a quick escape. Pig-like peccaries crash headlong through the bush, propelled by slender legs and tiny hooves, while agoutis and pacas – large rodents – are even faster, with the upright stance and bounding run of a hare. For humans, running through the scrub is asking for trouble. Not only does it contain squat, ground-hugging cacti, but also some of the biggest concentrations of poisonous snakes in the world.

Despite these perils, the Gran Chaco is not all wilderness. Much is grazing land and parts, particularly in Paraguay, have been transformed by the diligence of Mennonite Christians, who started settling there in the 1920s. The first Mennonite settlers came from Canada, and were later joined by co-religionists fleeing persecution in the former Soviet Union. Through a combination of hard work and careful agricultural research, they were extremely successful in growing crops and raising livestock in the areas they colonised. According to some estimates, Mennonite farms now provide about half of the dairy products consumed in Paraguay.

Bañados del Izozog

The south-western edge of the Gran Chaco is the region's highest, driest and least populated zone; in some places, whole years can go by without rain. But one part of western Chaco stays green all

THE LARGEST MAMMAL UNIQUE TO THE CHACO IS

the Chacoan peccary (*Catagonus wagneri*), measuring up to 69 cm tall at the shoulder and weighing up to 43 kg. It was long thought to be extinct until rediscovered in 1975.

PREHISTORIC 'TERROR BIRDS', the phorusrhacids, were related to the seriema. Up to 3 m tall, these powerful flightless South American predators could tear an anteater to shreds with their claws and beaks.

TEN OR MORE SPECIES OF ARMADILLO

live in the Gran Chaco, more than anywhere else in the world.

FACTS

The result is a lush inland delta, home to all kinds of animals, from giant river otters to rare hyacinth macaws. The swamp has just one outflow: unusually for a Chaco river, it trickles northwards and eventually joins a tributary of the Amazon. The rest of the swamp's water either soaks away into the ground or disappears in the heat of the Sun.

During the 1930s, war broke out in the northern Chaco between Bolivia and Paraguay, following reports that the region contained large reserves of oil. As it turned out, the reports were false and no oil was found, but the conflict caused around 100 000 casualties – more from malaria and other diseases than actual fighting – and left both countries close to economic ruin. But the absence of oil did have one positive side-effect: it saved the Bañados del Izozog from invasion by the outside world. In 2001, the swamp was listed as a Ramsar site – registered under the Ramsar Convention, which seeks to conserve the world's most important wetlands.

Another conservation initiative was launched in 1995 with the creation of the Kaa-Iya del Gran Chaco National Park, a region of tropical dry forest, also in Bolivia. This is a very different kind of landscape to rain forest, but still rich in wildlife. The park is home to an estimated 1000 jaguars, as well as other cat species, including pumas and ocelots. Among those who fought for the creation of Kaa-Iya were three local indigenous groups – the Isoseño-Guaraní, Chiquitano and Ayoreo. All three groups benefit from the preservation of a habitat where they can sustain their traditional way of life by hunting, river fishing and small-scale subsistence farming.

year round. It is known as the Bañados del Izozog – the name is a mixture of Spanish and the language of the local Guaraní people and literally means 'the bathing place where waters disappear'.

The water that irrigates this remote Bolivian oasis comes from high up in the Andes. After descending from the mountains, it heads out across the Gran Chaco, but instead of continuing eastwards to the Atlantic, it meets a huge natural depression, where the water fans out in countless slow-moving streams.

LONG-LEGGED WOLF The maned wolf is one of the Chaco's largest hunters. With extra-long legs, it stands 1 m high at the shoulder – a big advantage for a hunter searching an area for food.

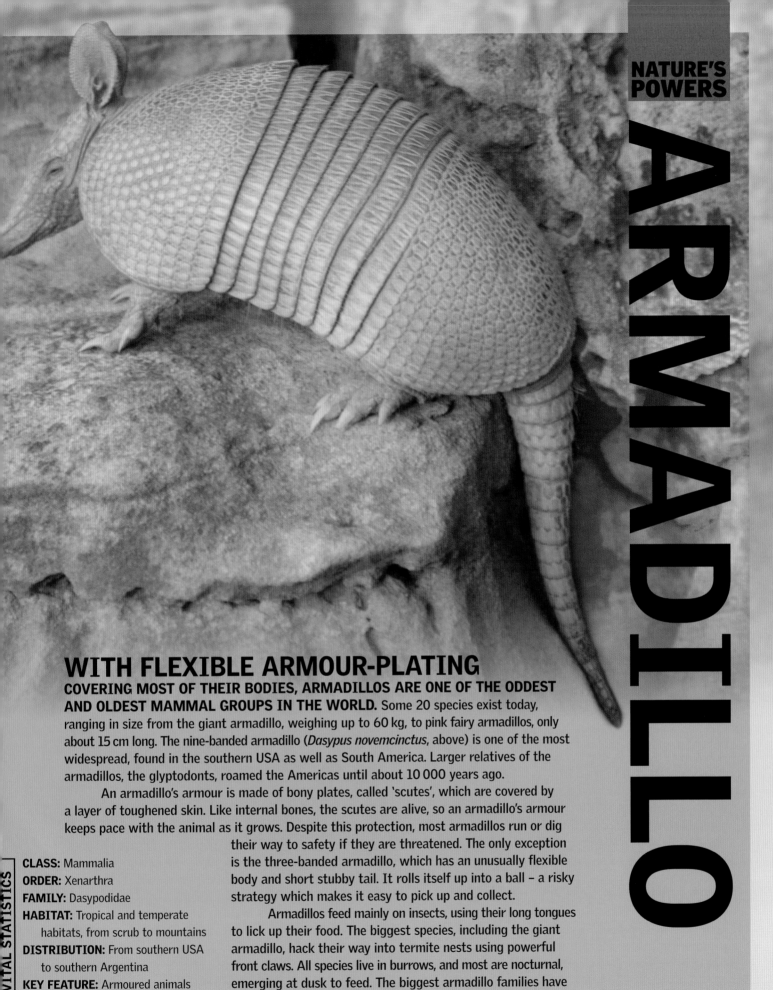

ARMADILLO

WITH FLEXIBLE ARMOUR-PLATING

COVERING MOST OF THEIR BODIES, ARMADILLOS ARE ONE OF THE ODDEST AND OLDEST MAMMAL GROUPS IN THE WORLD. Some 20 species exist today, ranging in size from the giant armadillo, weighing up to 60 kg, to pink fairy armadillos, only about 15 cm long. The nine-banded armadillo (*Dasypus novemcinctus*, above) is one of the most widespread, found in the southern USA as well as South America. Larger relatives of the armadillos, the glyptodonts, roamed the Americas until about 10 000 years ago.

An armadillo's armour is made of bony plates, called 'scutes', which are covered by a layer of toughened skin. Like internal bones, the scutes are alive, so an armadillo's armour keeps pace with the animal as it grows. Despite this protection, most armadillos run or dig their way to safety if they are threatened. The only exception is the three-banded armadillo, which has an unusually flexible body and short stubby tail. It rolls itself up into a ball – a risky strategy which makes it easy to pick up and collect.

Armadillos feed mainly on insects, using their long tongues to lick up their food. The biggest species, including the giant armadillo, hack their way into termite nests using powerful front claws. All species live in burrows, and most are nocturnal, emerging at dusk to feed. The biggest armadillo families have 12 young, but most females give birth to an average of four.

VITAL STATISTICS

CLASS: Mammalia
ORDER: Xenarthra
FAMILY: Dasypodidae
HABITAT: Tropical and temperate habitats, from scrub to mountains
DISTRIBUTION: From southern USA to southern Argentina
KEY FEATURE: Armoured animals found only in the Americas

WORLD'S END FORESTS

SOME 3000 KM SOUTH OF THE GRAN CHACO, THE FORESTS OF TIERRA DEL FUEGO BATTLE AGAINST SUB-ANTARCTIC WINDS. In sheltered places, trees can grow more than 20 m tall, but on exposed coasts they barely reach human head height before winter storms prune them back.

Lying at the sharp end of South America's 'southern cone', these are the southernmost forests on Earth, dominated by species from the southern beech family – the Nothofagaceae. They include the ñire or keterna – one of the smallest of the southern beeches, with scalloped, bright green leaves – and the lenga or hanis, which is taller with grey bark and graceful spreading branches. Although some southern beeches are evergreen, both these species lose their leaves in the autumn. Spring arrives in Tierra del Fuego in September, and then after the long days of

midsummer, autumn is underway by March. The southern beeches and other forest trees flare up in beautiful shades of orange, yellow and a deep coppery red, before dropping their leaves. Winter is a time of almost unrelieved bleakness, as the trees are swept by relentless gales and wind-driven snow.

Given this desolate scenery, it seems extraordinary that Tierra del Fuego's forests have any human history. But native Fuegians – the Yaghan or Yámana (see page 154) – lived here for thousands of years before the region was discovered by Europeans. The Yaghan used forest trees to make shelters and fishing canoes. They wore very little clothing, even during the coldest

FLEETING FLARE Dressed in their autumn colours, southern beeches decorate a mountainside in Tierra del Fuego. In cold conditions, the trees grow slowly, but can reach a great age.

In the 19th century, naturalists were astonished to find southern beeches in widely scattered parts of the world. About ten species grow in South America, four in New Zealand and three in Australia. More startling still, some grow in the tropical forests of New Caledonia and New Guinea – it is hard to imagine a starker contrast than between these forests and those on Tierra del Fuego. At the time, scientists thought that the continents were fixed in position, which made this kind of pattern extremely hard to explain. Then, as late as the 1960s, geologists accepted the theory that the continents are actually on the move. Their speed averages just a few centimetres a year – still fast enough to separate plants or animals that originally evolved in the same part of the world.

Experts now believe that the first southern beeches evolved in Gondwana, an ancient supercontinent that included today's New Zealand, Australia, Antarctica and South America. When Gondwana eventually split up, its separate parts carried their trees with them – the ancestors of the forests that exist today. As Antarctica travelled south, its climate chilled and its forests gradually lost the fight for survival. But beneath the ice, evidence survives that the continent was once forested. Among the fossils found there are leaves and stems of southern beeches, lasting relics of the most isolated forests in the world.

CRIMSON BEAUTIES Chile's south-western coast is the original home of many garden plants, including this species of fuchsia, Fuchsia magellanica. *In the wild, the flowers are pollinated by hummingbirds, which get dabbed with pollen as the birds feed.*

time of the year, and their only source of heat when afloat came from small fires, which they lit on beds of sand to prevent the canoes from catching fire. Although most of their food came from the sea, they also hunted land animals and harvested a bright orange fungus that sprouts from Fuegian trees.

Beeches in fjordland

Farther north, southern beeches also dominate the forests of the southern Andes. On Chile's south-western coast, they grow in one of the world's most dramatic fjord landscapes, where sea and shore intertwine in a maze of deep dark waterways. In almost 600 km of coastline there are only two major towns, while behind the coast the Andes rise steeply towards Patagonia's twin icefields, almost always hidden in the clouds. In this wild country, condors swoop low over the coast, and guanacos – smaller relatives of the llama and alpaca – follow tracks across the rocky terrain. Along the shore, blood-sucking horseflies are common, a feature that dissuades many travellers from lingering.

LOST
HORIZONS

6

IN THE WORLD OF WILD PLACES, FLAT DOES NOT MEAN DULL. Far from it, because level landscapes can create a feeling of seemingly endless space that is hard to match in hillier regions. Some of these places are half way between land and water: shallow lagoons like these (left) in India's Rann of Kutch, attracting feeding flamingos, or level plains of salty silt drying in the tropical sun. Flat landscapes include an extraordinary variety of much drier scenery, from scrub-covered deserts, with a disorienting lack of landmarks, to vast plateaus walled around by some of the world's highest mountain chains, or huge sweeps of grassland sprinkled with isolated trees. All of these places have one thing in common – far-reaching views towards a distant and uncluttered horizon, which often looks razor-sharp against the sky.

SPEEDING TO SAFETY Light coats and dark manes distinguish these wild asses from domesticated donkeys. These animals are in prime condition, after several months of abundant food following the annual monsoon.

THE RANN OF KUTCH

IN NORTH-EAST INDIA CLOSE TO THE PAKISTAN BORDER LIES ONE OF THE WORLD'S FLATTEST AND LONELIEST LANDSCAPES, where wild asses and migratory birds are among the few signs of life. The Rann of Kutch – 'rann' means a desert salt marsh – was once a shallow inlet of the Arabian Sea, but today this vast plain of silt floods for just a few months each year. Until the 20th century, few outsiders had visited this desolate region. One British military officer who saw the Rann in the 1820s described it as 'a space without counterpart on the globe ... where the sun shines with a deadly whiteness'.

Even today, the Rann of Kutch is remarkable for its sheer emptiness. More than a billion people live in the Indian subcontinent, but the Rann's 25 000 km² remain largely deserted. Apart from low-lying islands called bets, the shimmering mudflats stretch away towards a bare horizon.

The Rann's wild asses have a maximum speed of 70 km/h – the fastest of any member of the horse family – and they can cruise at 50 km/h, which beats the top running speed of many other grazing mammals.

LORDLY GAZE The nilgai or blue bull is Asia's biggest antelope. In India, religious tradition protects it from hunting, and mature males like this one can weigh over a quarter of a tonne.

Asia's wild asses

From a distance, the Rann's largest animals, Asian wild asses, look like little more than tiny dark specks against the expansive landscape. These large grazers are sturdily built, with two-tone coats, a short dark mane and a conspicuous dark stripe running down their backs. Getting close to them is not easy, because they are extremely wary, and their swiftness and stamina are legendary. They have a maximum speed of 70 km/h – the fastest of any member of the horse family – and they can cruise at 50 km/h, which beats the top running speed of many other grazing mammals.

These wild asses are a world away from the domesticated donkeys that are so common throughout the Indian subcontinent. Donkeys are descended from African asses – slow-moving, sure-footed animals that are critically endangered in the wild. The asses of the Rann are a separate species – the Asian wild ass, which has probably never been tamed. There are six kinds of Asian wild ass and all of them have been fighting a losing battle against hunters, and against farm animals that compete with them for food. The asses in the Rann of Kutch are no exception: today, there are only about 2000 left, and these salt flats are their last stronghold. Happily, their fight for survival is moving in the right direction. Despite periodic setbacks, their numbers have doubled in the last 40 years.

Seasonal visitors

For eight months of every year, the Rann dries out in the heat, and there is barely a trace of rain. Even so, it is not absolutely dry. In places, the sun beats down on shrunken rivers and brackish lakes, where birds of all kinds congregate to find food. Many of these birds are year-round residents, but in winter they are joined by thousands of migrants escaping the cold conditions further north.

With so many birds sharing these small oases of water, different ways of feeding can make all the difference in finding enough to eat. Grebes dive down from the surface, using their feet like propellers to speed after finger-sized

FACTS

THE RANN OF KUTCH IS THE **WINTER HOME OF OVER 50 000 MIGRATING** birds, including the only migrating flamingos in the Indian subcontinent. Some of the overwintering species – such as the curlew sandpiper – come from as far away as the shores of the Arctic Ocean.

THE WILD ASS sanctuary in the Rann of Kutch is India's largest wildlife reserve, covering an area of almost 5000 km².

THE KUTCH REGION produces much of the table salt that is used throughout India.

FACTS

fish. Many ducks use a technique called dabbling, diving down to collect food from the muddy bottom. And then there are the waders, like herons and spoonbills, that walk into the water on long slender legs. Of all the Rann's birds, it is the pelicans that are best equipped for dealing with large fish. They use their beaks like scoops, thanks to an elastic pouch that can hold food together with several litres of water. When a pelican closes its beak, the pouch tightens up, the water drains out – and the fish disappear down the bird's throat.

Drought and flood

By March, the migratory birds have left, and the Rann's lakes and lagoons are shrinking fast. With so little water, this is the hungriest time of year. Hyenas and jackals hunt on the mudflats, and scavenge food from dead remains. One of the Rann's largest wild cats, the caracal, which looks like a bobcat or lynx, with black tufts on the tips of its ears, specialises in hunting birds.

In the open it can leap up and knock small birds out of the air, a feat that very few other ground-based predators can match.

Towards the end of June, the temperature peaks as the first huge storms spread up from the south, signalling the start of the annual monsoon. What was firm ground soon turns into glutinous mud and the region's rivers start to swell, transforming parts of the Rann into a series of shallow lakes and lagoons. At the same time, the monsoon wind fans the tide, driving the sea towards the shore. Land animals retreat to the islands, while boats that have been stranded for months start to refloat.

The boats are there for a reason, because with the monsoon, millions of prawns arrive in the shallows to mate and to spawn. The prawn season is a busy time for the Rann's scattered human inhabitants, and also for its water birds. But it does not last for long. By the time the year nears its end, the skies clear and the rains cease. Water levels drop, the silt dries out and the Rann of Kutch becomes a desert once more.

PAUSE FOR REFLECTION With a wingspan of nearly 3 m, great white pelicans are some of the Rann's largest birds. Despite their enormous beaks, they are superb fliers, soaring high up with their necks tucked into their chests.

CROSSED BY A ROAD NEARLY 1200 KM LONG, Australia's Nullarbor Plain is the biggest slab of limestone in the world. With only minor variations of landscape and vegetation, the plain covers an area one and a half times the size of England, splitting the southern part of Australia in two. The name Nullarbor comes from the Latin meaning 'no tree' – a perfect description for this vast expanse of salt-resistant scrub, which rarely grows above shoulder-height. Even by the standards of Australia's outback, the Nullarbor is flat and sparsely populated. Beneath the plain lies a vast network of caves that have yielded some fascinating relics from Australia's distant past.

Even when the Aborigines had Australia to themselves, the Nullarbor had few human inhabitants because surface water is so hard to find. In the central part of the plain, summer temperatures can reach 50°C, and when it does rain, the water soon disappears underground. Life is no easier where the Nullarbor meets the sea, because the limestone plain ends abruptly in sheer cliffs that make it almost impossible to reach the shore.

Nullarbor's animals

The most dangerous time to drive in the Nullarbor is at sunset, because this is when kangaroos and wallabies break their daytime rest and set off to find food. They bound out of the saltbush in the fading twilight, sometimes lazing on the tarmac to soak up its warmth. From time to time, drivers have to swerve around an even bigger hazard: herds of wild camels that march across the highway, before disappearing into the bush. Camels were imported in the 19th century and were used as pack animals in the Nullarbor, until trains and trucks took their place. Today, several thousand still live on the plain, and they have adapted to it

NULLARBOR

so well that they have become part of the Nullarbor wildlife scene. Kangaroos and camels can survive in the harsh conditions here because they get a lot of their water from their food. For many of Australia's animals – particularly forest-dwelling ones – the Nullarbor is a no-go zone. The koala, for example, lives in the forests of eastern Australia, but this marsupial has never managed to spread to forests in the continent's west, because the treeless Nullarbor stands in its way.

The Nullabor is so big that even birds can find it difficult to make the crossing between east and west. In the early 20th century, Australian bird-lovers sometimes gave their favourite species a helping hand, carrying them westwards by train or by ship. Two of these birds – the kookaburra and the sulphur-crested cockatoo – thrived once they were released and are now a common sight around Perth, over 1500 km west of their original home.

PLAIN

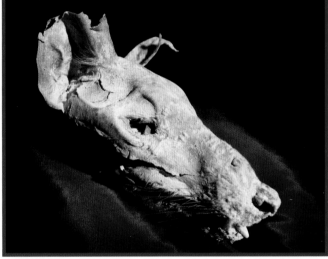

Under the surface

The Nullarbor's limestone formed about 25 million years ago, under a shallow seabed. Later, when it was raised above sea level, the rock was gradually gnawed away by rain, creating one of the world's biggest network of caves. Today, the Nullarbor is dry, but some of its caves are permanently flooded with water that has been there for thousands of years.

These flooded caves attract cave-divers from all over the world. In 1983, a French team set a new world record when they swam and crawled over 6 km through Cocklebiddy Cave. Nearly 20 years later, the caves again made headlines when another team explored three dry caves about 100 km from the coast. After dropping down through the vertical entrance shafts, the divers made an astounding discovery: all around them were the bones of extinct animals – ones that had fallen through the cave mouths and died underground. Altogether, these natural traps yielded the remains of many extinct mammals, from giant kangaroos and wombats to *Thylacoleo*, a fearsome marsupial predator that was Australia's equivalent of the lion. In the subterranean stillness, their fossilised skeletons were beautifully preserved, despite being up to 800 000 years old.

LONG ROAD AHEAD Unsurfaced tracks cut across parts of the Nullarbor, leading to remote sheep stations in the bush.

SEAS OF GRASS

SEASON'S END Mongolia's grassland is a place of extremes – warm in summer and often bitterly cold in winter.

GRASSLAND FORMS WHERE IT IS NOT DRY ENOUGH FOR DESERT, BUT IS TOO DRY FOR MOST TREES. Long ago, huge expanses of natural grassland existed in every continent except Antarctica, but that changed with the invention of the plough. The world's natural grasslands have been shrinking ever since as more and more of them are ploughed for crops. But in some places, such as Mongolia, South Africa and South America, large swathes of natural grassland survive, all sharing uncluttered horizons and wide-open skies. Many people find these open spaces energising and uplifting – a feeling that may date back to our distant past, when humans roamed grasslands like these in search of food.

A natural partnership

Grasses first evolved about 60 million years ago. Ever since then, grazing mammals have helped grasslands to thrive. Grazers do this by biting off grass close to the ground – something that looks like fatal damage, but in fact, the opposite is true. Grass can survive this kind of treatment, but saplings cannot. As a result, grazing mammals prevent shrubs from growing in grassland, which allows the grasses to dominate.

This natural partnership is so successful that grassland supports the biggest herds of wild animals on Earth. In East Africa, they include hundreds of thousands of zebras, as well as

several million antelope. Many of them keep on the move throughout the year, following an age-old cycle that marches in step with the climate, and the life-giving rains. In colder parts of the world, grass often dies back to ground level, but below the surface, most plants stay alive. As soon as spring arrives, they start sprouting once more, and the yellowish hues of the winter landscape turn into a carpet of luxuriant green.

Until the mid-1800s, North America's grasslands – the prairies – were home to over 60 million bison, creating trails as big as motorways as the herds migrated across the landscape. South Africa's grasslands, known as the veld, were grazed by even bigger herds of springboks, some of them containing over 10 million animals. Both bison and springbok suffered appallingly at the hands of hunters after the arrival of Europeans, but fortunately the slaughter stopped just before either species became extinct.

An open stage

Where so many grazing animals go, predators naturally follow. In Africa, the cheetah is one of the few large grassland hunters that operates right out in the open, in full view of its prey. Instead of trying to conceal itself, it relies on its incredible sprinting ability

to run down its food. In contrast, lions and leopards are poor at hunting in close-cropped grass, where they can be spotted from far away. Instead, they do most of their hunting at night, or in places where tall grass helps to conceal them. They can be noisy killers – something that attracts hyenas and other scavengers, hoping for a share.

Only a few grazing animals are capable of fighting back against determined killers like these. The large, powerful Cape buffalo are amongst the most fearsome – they have been known to kill lions and also humans, using their massive horns that span up to 1.2 m from tip to tip. For most grazers, though, the keys to survival are vigilance and speed. Antelopes constantly check the horizon for signs of danger, and so do some of the most characteristic animals in grasslands: giant flightless birds.

Grassland birds

It is no accident that the biggest birds living in grassland are all ones that cannot fly. Largest of all is the African ostrich, which stands 2 m high and can weigh as much as 120 kg. Australia's emus are only slightly shorter, followed by South America's rheas. All have long necks and legs, but their wings are so weak that they have no hope of getting into the air. It sounds like a recipe for disaster, but nature has equipped them with other ways of looking after themselves and their young.

Ostriches have the biggest eyes of any bird, measuring 5 cm in diameter, and their position – high up on a tremendously long neck – gives them a superb view of the horizon. At the first hint of danger, ostriches stop feeding and start to make their getaway. Their immense thighs power enormous strides over 5 m long, with their hoof-like claws pounding into the ground. At top speed, an ostrich can hit around 70 km/h – the fastest speed for any bird on land. And should one get cornered, it has a fearsome weapon of last resort: it can lash out with its powerful legs,

PECKING ORDER Lesser rheas peck up seeds and insects from stubbly grass in Argentina.

LOOKOUT POST A rocky outcrop or kopje gives these lions a good view over the grass in Tanzania's Serengeti National Park. Early in the dry season, the grass is still green.

ripping forwards and downwards with its claws. Emus and rheas are not quite as fast as ostriches, but they are amazingly adept at escaping when a predator starts closing in.

Unlike other birds, these grassland residents behave much more like the grazing mammals that are their neighbours, often feeding alongside them too. Mammals may stir up insects when they eat, which the birds snap up, along with all sorts of other food, from lizards and spiders to seeds. In return, the birds are efficient sentries, keeping both eyes on the horizon for any signs of danger.

Workers among the grass

Other large animals that make their home in grasslands include elephants, rhinos, antelopes and some of the world's largest lizards and snakes. But not everything here is supersized. In the tropics, ant-like termites play an important part in the recycling system, feeding on dead grass or wood, which they collect after dark. Worker termites are only a few millimetres long, but in some kinds of grassland, they are so numerous that they outweigh all the grazing animals put together.

Termites are among nature's most talented builders, with each species constructing its own kind of nest. In East Africa, macrotermites build giant towers of sunbaked clay that can be 9 m high and 2 m across. In northern Australia, magnetic termites build nests that look like tombstones – the tallest of them over 2.5 m high. Each 'tombstone' is aligned in a

north–south direction, so that its flat sides catch the warmth of the rising and setting sun. At midday, the nest is edge-on to the Sun, which helps to keep it cool. Like Africa's termite towers, these nests are even bigger than they look, because the inhabited part of the nest is underground.

Giant grasses

There are nearly 10 000 kinds of grass in the world. Most grow to less than knee-high, but some can be huge. Excluding bamboos, one of the biggest is elephant grass, which grows up to 5 m high in damp ground in tropical Africa, where elephants love its soft, nutritious stems. And in northern India, the rare Asian rhino hides in the giant grass that grows in swampy ground. After the rainy season, when the grass is fully grown, the only way to catch a glimpse of these rhinos is on elephant-back.

Giant grasses also grow in some colder parts of the world. One of the best known is pampas grass – a tall grass native to the windswept grassland of Patagonia. The grass has narrow leaves with razor-sharp edges and silvery flower heads up to 4 m high, which can produce over a million seeds. Pampas grass was admired by Victorian plant-hunters, who introduced it to many other parts of the world. For small animals, pampas grass doubles as a source of food and as a home. The same is true of tussac grass, which grows on islands in the Southern Ocean. Tussac grass may not be the most elegant plant, but it is one of the toughest, offering shelter against the wind behind some of the world's bleakest shorelines. Penguins make their burrows underneath it, and fur seals often give birth in hollows between the clumps – a good way of keeping their young out of the chilly wind.

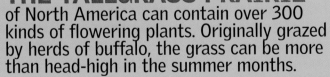

WITH AN AVERAGE ALTITUDE OF OVER 3000 M, SOUTH AMERICA'S ALTIPLANO IS THE HIGHEST PLATEAU IN THE WESTERN HEMISPHERE. Flanked by the snow-capped Andes, the region contains wide stony plains, and two giant lakes that once formed part of an inland sea. Altiplano means 'high plain' – a name given to the region in the 16th century by Spanish conquistadors, who were the first outsiders to travel across the plateau. In many ways what they saw has changed little today: few trees grow this high up, and the views are often spectacularly sharp in the crystal-clear mountain air. Where there is enough soil, farmers grow crops for themselves and their families, but elsewhere the ground is too rocky for anything but grass. This is grazed by herds of llamas and alpacas, which roam as high as 4500 m in their search for food. These high-altitude animals were domesticated more than 6000 years ago, and as free-roaming animals, they are found nowhere else in the world.

The Altiplano lies in the tropics, so the Sun is always high in the sky. But even so, the local people are often well wrapped up against the cold. The thin air does not retain heat, and the thermometer plummets as soon as the Sun sets. By dawn, pails of water left outside are often covered by a skin of ice.

ANCIENT CRAFT A fisherman poles a boat made of Lake Titicaca's totora reeds. The boats have changed little over hundreds of years.

HARVEST TIME Lake Titicaca reeds are actually a kind of sedge with creeping underwater roots.

THE ALTIPLANO

The high life

The Altiplano begins in Peru and curves in an arc southwards through Bolivia to northern Argentina, a distance of over 1000 km. During the last Ice Age, the entire plateau was buried by glaciers, but when the ice melted, over 10 000 years ago, the Altiplano filled with a huge lake up to 300 m deep. Ever since then, this prehistoric lake has been slowly drying out. Today, two large remnants are left: Lake Poopó, in Bolivia, and Lake Titicaca, which straddles the border between Bolivia and Peru at an altitude of 3812 m. Covering over 8000 km^2, Lake Titicaca is by far the biggest and deepest of the two and works like an enormous solar heater, soaking up the energy in sunshine and warming the land nearby. Thanks to this, farmers are able to grow crops that would otherwise struggle to survive so high up.

Lake Titicaca's shoreline is mainly steep and rocky, but parts of it are covered with giant reeds, which the local Uros Indians use to make boats and houses. They also use them to make floating islands – a tradition that started over 500 years ago as a defence against Inca invaders. The reeds have spongy stems that make them naturally buoyant, but when they are cut and left underwater, they gradually rot away. To prevent their islands from sinking, the Uros keep adding fresh reeds above the waterline, which can keep them floating for as long as 25 years.

Lake Titicaca's reeds provide a valuable habitat for a wide range of wildlife, including species of native fish, which lay their eggs among them. One of the lake's most intriguing residents is the Lake Titicaca frog, a giant amphibian up to 30 cm long whose skin is arranged in folds, like a loosely fitting bag. The frog spends its life underwater, where its ample skin enables it to absorb sufficient oxygen. The reedbeds are also home to some remarkable water birds, including wafer-thin rails, whose bodies easily slip between the reed stems, and the stubby-winged Titicaca flightless grebe, which breeds among the reeds and hardly ever comes ashore.

HIMALAYAS

THE HIMALAYAS ARE MUCH MORE THAN THE GREATEST CHAIN OF MOUNTAINS IN THE WORLD. North of the great peaks, they also form the world's highest and largest plateau, covering an area equivalent to the whole of western Europe. Although people have lived on the Himalayan plateau for thousands of years, the landscape is so tough and unyielding that settlements have always been sparse. With only about two or three frost-free months each summer, the growing season is very short. Instead of growing food, many of the plateau's people herd yaks, which provide meat, milk, wool and dung – the four staples of daily life. Yak wool is soft and downy, and can be easily spun into yarn for clothing. In a landscape with almost no trees, yak dung is a valuable resource – when it is dry, it can be collected and used as a fuel.

There are several million yaks in captivity, but unlike cattle, this species still exists in the wild. In spring and summer, wild yaks, which can weigh up to 1200 kg, feed on mountain pastures up to altitudes of 6000 m – higher than any other large grazing mammal. Apart from human hunters, their main enemies are wolves. A wolf pack cannot bring down an adult yak, but it will pursue a herd in the hope of catching a calf.

SLOW CLIMB Heading towards basecamp on Mount Everest, a train of heavily laden yaks is framed by the stunning backdrop of Nepal's Sagarmatha National Park.

The Himalayan plateau's high-altitude grassland is also home to snow leopards and the rare chiru, or Tibetan antelope. The chiru is famous for its extraordinarily fine hair, which provides the antelope with insulation at heights similar to those reached by the larger yak. Traditionally, the chiru has been killed for its wool, which is woven into the ultra-soft luxury fabric 'shahtoosh', and it is now endangered.

Lakes in the sky

Despite its dry climate, the Himalayan plateau is the source of some of the largest rivers in southern Asia, including the Ganges, the Mekong and the Yangtze. They are fed by streams among the Himalayan peaks, which swell with monsoon rain. Further north, in the rain shadow cast by the mountains, many rivers flow for hundreds of kilometres across the open plateau, before ending in isolated lakes. Many of these lakes are traditional places of pilgrimage, where the faithful bathe in icy water, or make the long walk around the entire lake shore.

Some Himalayan lakes are vast, with names that are as evocative as their locations. Lake Manasarovar, in south-west Tibet, is one of the world's highest freshwater lakes, at over 4550 m. At this altitude, the clear, dry air gives its water an incredibly pure shade of blue. Its water helps to feed the River Indus, which flows out of the Himalayas through Pakistan, and then into the Indian Ocean. Nearly 2000 km to the north-east, on the opposite edge of the plateau, Qinghai Lake is the largest body of water in

AUTUMN SHADES The sacred Mount Kailash in Tibet looms over the shores of Lake Manasarovar. The lake freezes over during the winter months before melting again in spring. Bathing in the lake and drinking its water is believed to cleanse all sins.

China. Unlike Manasarovar, it does not have any natural outlets, and its water is slightly salty. Its level constantly changes: at present, it is falling by several centimetres a year.

High-altitude flight

Much of the Himalayan plateau is covered by steppe grassland – a habitat that is dry, harsh and cold for much of the year. Thanks to its rivers and lakes, it is also a prime breeding site for some of the world's highest-flying geese and swans. In Asia, the mute swan breeds around the edges of the Himalayan plateau, spending the winter in lowland China.

Another high-flyer, the bar-headed goose, breeds on high-altitude lakes in Central Asia, and spends the winter in marshy ground in northern India. To get between their winter and summer homes, the geese face a gigantic obstacle: the main wall of the Himalayan range. The birds travel in flocks, flying through mountain passes where they can. But sometimes they have to fly right over the mountains that lie on their route. One flock was seen flying over Mount Everest at an altitude of 9375 m – a record for a migratory bird.

Despite its dry climate, the Himalayan plateau is the source of some of the largest rivers in southern Asia, including the Ganges, the Mekong and the Yangtze.

FRESHWATER
WILDERN

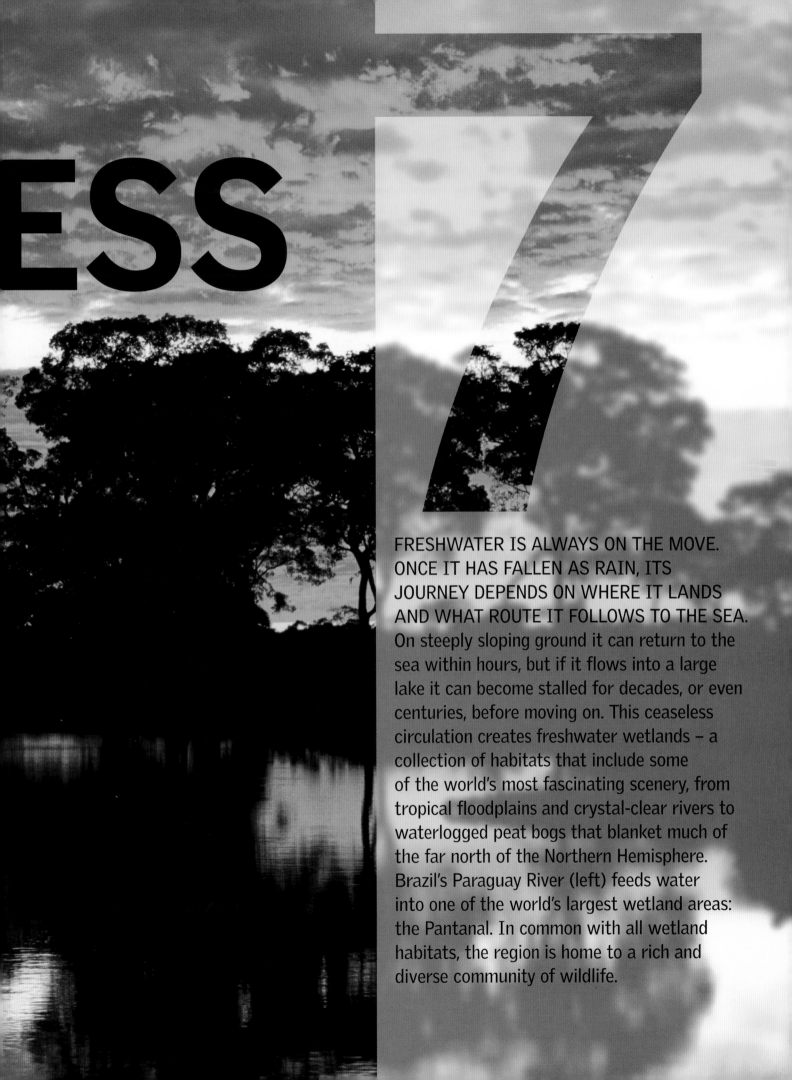

ESS

7

FRESHWATER IS ALWAYS ON THE MOVE. ONCE IT HAS FALLEN AS RAIN, ITS JOURNEY DEPENDS ON WHERE IT LANDS AND WHAT ROUTE IT FOLLOWS TO THE SEA. On steeply sloping ground it can return to the sea within hours, but if it flows into a large lake it can become stalled for decades, or even centuries, before moving on. This ceaseless circulation creates freshwater wetlands – a collection of habitats that include some of the world's most fascinating scenery, from tropical floodplains and crystal-clear rivers to waterlogged peat bogs that blanket much of the far north of the Northern Hemisphere. Brazil's Paraguay River (left) feeds water into one of the world's largest wetland areas: the Pantanal. In common with all wetland habitats, the region is home to a rich and diverse community of wildlife.

STILL
WATERS

ANCIENT LINE-UP Finland's Lake Pielinen reflects the sun. Like many of Finland's lakes, Pielinen is aligned north-west to south-east along the route of long-gone glaciers.

SEEN FROM THE AIR, FINLAND'S FORESTED INTERIOR GLINTS LIKE A SERIES OF POLISHED MIRRORS as lake after lake reflects the sunlight. Despite its small size, Finland has nearly 200 000 lakes larger than 5 hectares – one for every 25 inhabitants. This extraordinary landscape is the work of glaciers, which scraped out hollows in the underlying rock. As the glaciers retreated, the hollows filled with meltwater.

Other countries in the northern reaches of the Northern Hemisphere also have extensive glacial lakes: Minnesota in the US is known as the 'Land of 10 000 Lakes', while both northern Canada and Siberia have so many they are impossible to count. Many of the lakes are in such remote places that they see very few human visitors, and even in summer the water can be icy cold.

MINERAL RICH Tiwu Nuwa Muri Koo Fia, or the Lake of Young Men and Maidens, is one of three coloured lakes on Kelimutu, a volcano on Flores, Indonesia. The colour may be caused by minerals, bacteria, or geological processes.

The lake-makers

Some of the most powerful forces on Earth are responsible for lakes, and they work on varied timetables. Finland's lakes took thousands of years to form as the glaciers slowly shrunk back. Others are created almost instantly when earthquakes shift huge quantities of earth and rock to block river valleys, or volcanic eruptions create deep craters. The colour of crater lakes varies: some are as clear as glass, while others are deep green or yellowish brown. Blue Lake, in South Australia, changes colour throughout the year. In summer, calcium carbonate in the warm surface water crystallises and scatters blue lightwaves to produce a brilliant cobalt blue; in winter, the water is steely grey.

Some of the world's most remarkable lakes are shrouded in darkness. In limestone regions, rainwater percolates down through the ground, dissolving the rock as it goes and producing caverns that fill with gently flowing water. Most of these lakes are closed off from the outside world and not the slightest ripple betrays the fact that the water is moving. One of the largest known is in the Dragon's Breath Cave in Namibia, covering more than 2 hectares, but there could be even larger subterranean lakes waiting to be discovered.

Freshwater giants

The time water takes to flow through a lake is called its residence time; the bigger the lake, the longer the time. Many lakes hold water for 20–50 years, but this is a short stay compared to the heavyweights of the freshwater world. Lake Superior in Canada is fed by 200 major rivers and has the largest surface area of any lake on Earth: it has a residence time of nearly two centuries – a result of its vast area and its average depth of nearly 150 m. Only two lakes contain more water: Lake Tanzania in Africa's Great Rift Valley, and Russia's Lake Baikal – at 1700 m the deepest lake in the world.

HIDDEN WATERS Most underground lakes are in limestone regions. Dzitnup Cenote, one of thousands in the Yucatán, is the only one in the region accessible to people.

SHIFTING STREAMS

WHEN RAIN TRICKLES DOWN A WINDOW-PANE, IT SEEMS TO WRIGGLE LIKE SOMETHING ALIVE. On a much larger scale, rivers and streams behave in a similar way, twisting and turning and changing direction as they travel towards the sea, cutting down through the underlying soil and rock and wearing away at the riverbanks. Most of the changes are small, but added up year after year they can have a big impact on the landscape. Riverbanks collapse, floods create sandbars and mudbanks, whole islands come and go.

Steep riverbanks provide animals with one of the safest locations for a nest, and mammals and birds burrow in, creating homes that are difficult for most predators to approach. Otters

RIVERBANK PREDATOR Mink are slim, fearsome hunters that can follow prey into small spaces, including tunnels above and below the waterline. They can even get into the burrows of water voles.

are among the largest burrowers, while the Australian platypus is far and away the oddest with its duck-like bill and broad, webbed feet. The platypus is typically found in billabongs – dark, stagnant oxbow lakes that are scattered along watercourses in the Australian bush. A breeding female digs an elaborate nesting burrow up to 20 m long, where she lays a clutch of two eggs.

While many riverbank animals are highly territorial – a male otter or platypus will not tolerate another male setting up

BEAUTIFUL NUISANCE The pretty flowers of Himalayan balsam produce explosive seedpods that scatter the seeds up to 5 m away, helping the plant to spread swiftly along riverbanks.

home close by – others prefer safety in numbers. Sand martins, which dig burrows more than 1 m long in sandy or gravelly riverbanks, often nest in groups of a dozen or more burrows, while some bank swallows breed in colonies of more than 100 birds. Rosy bee-eaters, which prefer collapsed riverbanks, breed in immense numbers. A colony discovered in 1933 in a remote part of West Africa had over 25 000 nestholes. This bee-eater city was probably home to at least 40 000 birds.

Invasion routes

Rivers and streams provide highways for invading species, some of which spread so successfully that they cause the destruction of their new homes. In Europe, invaders include the coypu from South America and the North American signal crayfish, who tunnel into riverbanks and destroy riverside vegetation, increasing the speed of erosion and causing banks to collapse. Animals are not the only culprits: waterside plants can spread even faster. Himalayan balsam is now common along UK riverbanks, where it grows in such profusion in summer that it smothers other plants, leaving riverbanks completely bare in winter and at risk of erosion.

HOME DELIVERY A male European bee-eater feeds its mate as she reaches out of their nesting burrow. Once the nestlings have hatched, they stay in the tunnel for four weeks.

EVERGLADES

A VAST EXPANSE OF WETLANDS INHABITED BY FISH, ALLIGATORS, AND SOME OF THE CONTINENT'S MOST SPECTACULAR BIRDS, the Everglades covers about 13 000 km² of southern Florida between Lake Okeechobee and the sea.

Being in the sub-tropics, this part of the USA is drenched by over 1000 mm of rain each year. Lake Okeechobee works like a giant reservoir, gathering in the rain and then slowly releasing it to flow across the region's highly porous, water-holding limestone bedrock. During the wet summer months, when 75 per cent of the region's annual precipitation falls, the outflow from Lake Okeechobee reaches its peak, swelling into an immense sheet of water just a few centimetres deep but up to 80 km wide, draining towards Florida Bay.

Most trees, apart from swamp specialists such as the Baldcypress, have difficulty surviving in waterlogged conditions. Instead, the Everglades is dominated by sawgrass, a plant whose sharp-edged leaves can slice deep into unprotected skin. In the Everglades, the sawgrass swamp is sprinkled with small islands and pock-marked with shallow pools. Weaving through the swamps are channels of clearer flowing water, known as sloughs, that remain flooded most of the year.

During the winter dry season, when the water flow drops, the sawgrass loses its leaves, but with the arrival of the

DEADLY GAZE Crouched on a floating branch, a green-backed heron fixes its prey with a hypnotic stare. Its backward bending 'knees' are actually its ankles – the bird's true knees are hidden under its wings.

EASY RIDER Airboats are widely used in the Everglades, keeping people at a safe distance from the sharp-edged sawgrass. The leaves have saw-like teeth, which can be seen under a microscope (inset).

wet season the tallest stands of sawgrass can tower 3 m high. At this time of year, southern Florida's climate can feel uncomfortably humid, with thunderstorms building up in the afternoons. As the lightning flickers over a darkening sky, the sawgrass teems with mosquitoes, keeping even the most inquisitive visitors at bay.

Stalking the swamps

Sawgrass swamps are uncomfortable places for people, but they are tailor-made for wetland birds. One of the smallest is the green-backed heron, a furtive hunter that creeps along the edge of pools. Like other herons, it holds its neck hunched against its body, like a tightly squeezed letter 'S'. As it moves along the water's edge, its yellow eyes peer forwards, focusing just beyond its beak. If anything edible comes within range, its beak darts forwards, impaling its prey before it has a chance to hop or swim away.

Green-backed herons are not much bigger than a crow, but with so much food at or below the waterline, the Everglades is also home to some of the giants of the heron family. The great blue heron is up to 1.4 m long, with a wingspan that is half as big again. Despite being a good flier, it spends little time in the air. Instead, it wades into pools and waits motionless but

vigilant, sometimes for over an hour at a time. This method of fishing is harder than it looks, and young birds take months to learn the patience and accuracy of their parents. It can also be dangerous, because herons are not the only animals searching for food.

The Everglades is famous for alligators, but it is home to many bird-hunting predators, including the American crocodile and the highly venomous Florida cottonmouth. This semi-aquatic snake, a close relative of rattlesnakes, feeds mainly on fish, but will take young turtles, baby alligators and water birds. It can also give humans a fatal bite.

The Florida panther

Before the arrival of Spanish settlers, Native Americans avoided the Everglades with its resident snakes, mosquitoes and razor-edged vegetation. They settled instead on southern Florida's islands or along river mouths, where they could move about more easily on foot or by canoe. Today, park rangers often use airboats to cross the sawgrass, but at dusk the Everglades still has the same feeling of remoteness that it would have had hundreds of years ago, despite the fact that the busy city of Miami is only a short drive away. The Everglades has few large land mammals, as the going is so difficult, but dusk is the time of day when the

ALLIGATOR

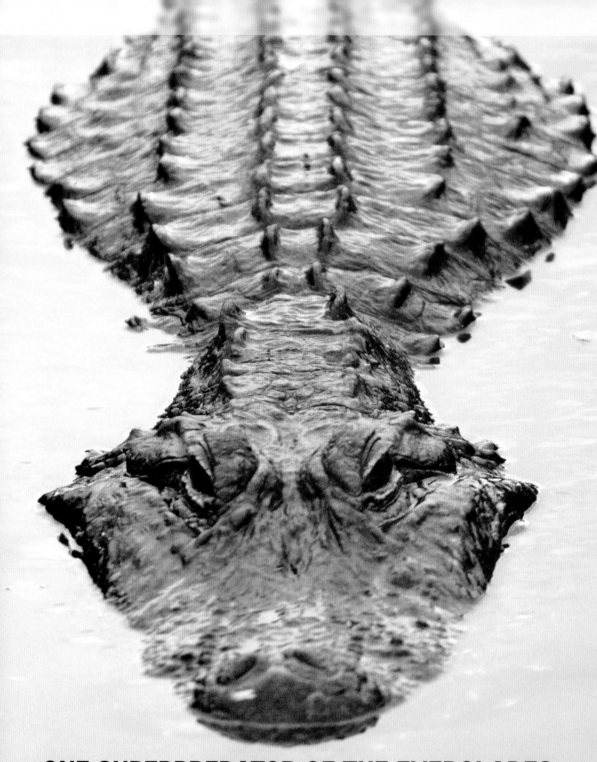

ONE SUPERPREDATOR OF THE EVERGLADES

HAS BEEN AROUND FOR HUNDREDS OF THOUSANDS OF YEARS. The American, or Mississippi, alligator once roamed as far north as Washington, DC, but the last ice age pushed it into the warmer south. Most adult alligators are under 5 m long, but the longest ever recorded measured 5.8 m from its snout to the tip of its tail. Unlike the American crocodile, alligators have rounded snouts and their lower teeth do not protrude. They eat almost anything, from fish and water birds to livestock that venture too close to the water's edge. In spring, mature females scrape together mounds of vegetation for a nest, and lay a clutch of about 20 eggs, which take about two months to hatch. Scattered across the Everglades are alligator holes, pits that they clear of vegetation and debris using their claws and tails. The holes retain water for most of the year, providing not only alligators but a range of aquatic creatures – including fish, snakes, turtles and birds – with a refuge during the dry season.

CLASS: Reptilia
ORDER: Crocodilia
SPECIES: *Alligator mississipiensis*
HABITAT: Lakes, freshwater swamps, canals
DISTRIBUTION: Coastal and inland from Maryland to south-east Texas
KEY FEATURE: Largest reptile in North America

VITAL STATISTICS

AIR BREATHER A favourite prey of alligators, the long-nosed gar can breathe by gulping air at the surface, which enables this fish to survive in the warm, stagnant water of the Everglades, where the oxygen level is low.

rarest of them, the Florida panther, comes out to hunt.

The name is misleading because it is not a panther (or jaguar) but a type of puma or cougar, originally found throughout the US Gulf states. Pumas typically weigh less than 100 kg, but they are incredibly strong for their size and can bring down prey several times their own weight – an ability that does not endear them to cattle farmers. There are records of attacks on people, and while few have been fatal they have helped to put the Florida panther high on the unwanted list. By the mid-1900s, only about 30 were left. In 1976, a recovery plan was launched to bring the panther back from the brink. The species seems to be making a slow recovery, but even so, there are fewer than 100 in the wild.

Tropical islands

Panthers can swim well, but like domestic cats they avoid getting wet. In the Everglades, where water is all around, they are restricted mainly to hammocks – the local name for low-lying islands, typically less than a metre high, but this is enough to keep them above water all year round. Varying in size from 0.4 to 40 hectares, hammocks are covered with hardwood forest that is the closest North America gets to tropical jungle. Hammocks often have dozens of different kinds of trees, including slender-trunked royal palms, West Indies mahogany and wild tamarind. Many of the trees are evergreen, with sharp 'drip tips' on their leaves that help rainwater to run off. Hammocks are also home to a species of strangler fig – the northernmost one in the Americas. The strangler grows from seeds dropped by birds high in the hammock. True to its name, it slowly chokes the life out of its host tree, then takes the host's place.

The animals of hammock forests are as colourful as any in the tropics. They include vividly coloured butterflies and bright green anole lizards, which scuttle over the ground or along treetrunks and branches. Green anoles can change colour to merge with their background, and the males have a flap of bright pink skin just below their chins, which they can extend like a signaller's flag.

With its flat topography, the Everglades is an ideal hunting ground for birds of prey, such as ospreys and bald eagles. Most nest high in the trees, so hammocks are a precious resource for them. Many also often return to a favourite perch once they have made a catch. Ospreys live entirely on fish, but bald eagles also eat mammals, reptiles and all kinds of dead remains. Like the osprey, this huge aerial predator, with a wingspan of over 2 m, often returns to the same nest year after year. Each time a pair of bald eagles breeds, they add more branches and sticks to their treetop pile. After many years of this patching-up process, a bald eagle nest can be as big as a family car. Many other birds of prey live in the Everglades, including the agile swallow-tailed kite and the snail kite.

OVER 200 SPECIES OF BIRDS ARE REGULARLY SEEN IN THE Everglades and a further 100 have been spotted there. Together this amounts to about a third of the total number of bird species found in the whole of North America.

3 CM per km is the average slope in the Everglades – so gentle that water can take a year to flow from Lake Okeechobee to the sea.

THE FLORIDA MANATEE IS THE LARGEST mammal in the Everglades, weighing up to 600 kg. FACTS

BACKWATERS AND BAYOUS

AN EERIE ATMOSPHERE HAUNTS THE SWAMP-FILLED FORESTS AND SLUGGISH BAYOUS, or streams, of the southern USA. Although less visited than the Everglades, these subtropical wetlands harbour almost as much wildlife. The dark, shady expanses of water and trees are festooned with Spanish moss – a plant that looks like grey-green hair and is almost synonymous with the Deep South and its humid summer climate.

Despite the name, Spanish moss is not a moss at all, but a flowering plant that spends all its life off the ground. It doesn't just grow on trees, but

SPEAR-FISHING The anhinga stabs fish with its sharp, pointed beak. It swims with its body submerged apart from its head and neck.

ALLIGATOR TERRITORY Spanish moss hangs from Baldcypress trees in Louisiana, creating shade and the perfect environment for lurking alligators.

also trails from wooden roofs and telephone wires, sometimes causing them to collapse. Spanish moss belongs to the bromeliads, a group of over 2000 mainly tropical species of varied size. It is an epiphyte, a plant that grows aboard another plant so that it can get a better share of daylight. Spanish moss is covered with tiny scales that absorb moisture from rain, and it collects nutrients from dust and fallen leaves. It has no need of soil provided that the climate is warm and damp. When Spanish moss is fully grown, it can be over a metre long, but its flowers are so small that they are invisible from the ground.

Trees with knees

Not many trees can survive with their roots permanently underwater, but the Baldcypress flourishes in the Deep South's swamps and shallow lakes. It is a type of redwood, but unlike most conifers it drops its leaves in autumn, leaving it 'bald' during the coldest and driest time of year. Baldcypresses do not simply tolerate water – they thrive in it. Given enough time, they can reach over 35 m high. Around the base of their trunks are narrow buttress roots that prop them up in waterlogged mud. In deeper water they are often surrounded by knobbly growths called 'cypress knees'. The knees stick up a few centimetres above the waterline – just enough to absorb oxygen from the air. The oxygen travels to the tip of every root, enabling the roots to grow in the oxygen-starved water and mud.

Reptile habitat

In the sluggish waters of the bayous, dozens of different reptiles lie in wait for prey. Alligators are common in this habitat, as are some highly poisonous snakes. At the first sign of trouble harmless watersnakes swim away, but venomous copperheads and cottonmouths stand their ground.

North America has a large number of freshwater turtles and terrapins, and many of them live in the bayous and quiet backwaters of the Deep South. Musk turtles feed on the bottom, where their well-camouflaged shells make the turtles difficult to spot. Many of the freshwater turtles are not much bigger than a hand even when fully grown. By comparison, the alligator snapping turtle is immense, with a record weight of over 100 kg. This enormous reptile lurks at the bottom of lakes or rivers with its mouth open, wriggling a pink flap of flesh that looks like a worm. If a fish swims close to investigate, the turtle snaps its jaws shut, often slicing its prey in two.

TESTING THE AIR A Florida cottonmouth flicks out its tongue, tasting the air for the scent of prey. A good swimmer, it grows up to 1.2 m long and has a highly poisonous bite.

OVERLEAF Redbelly turtles like to bask in the sun. They crowd onto rocks or fallen trees, but plop back into the water at any sign of danger. These ones are being watched by an anhinga.

EVERY NOVEMBER, THE RIVER PARAGUAY BURSTS ITS BANKS, RECHARGING ONE OF THE WORLD'S LARGEST WETLANDS – a vast area of tropical grassland known as the Pantanal. Shared by three countries – Paraguay, Bolivia and Brazil – the Pantanal comprises over 100 000 km² of flooded land in the wet season.

The floods trigger the start of the breeding season for many of the Pantanal's animals, from caimans to tropical birds. The water comes mainly from Brazil's highlands, which drain westwards towards the River Paraguay. Even in the dry season the Paraguay is immense, but during the rainy season it floods so extensively that the river itself disappears. Apart from ribbons of tropical forest and scattered hills, the entire landscape is submerged. No one travels if they can avoid it, and the area is effectively shut off from the outside world.

While people stay close to home, the Pantanal's freshwater inhabitants make full use of the expansion in living space. Fish swim through gates and fences, chased by the largest otters in the world. Green anacondas glide through the waterlogged vegetation, searching for plant-eating capybaras and fish-eating birds. And after months of being trapped in shallow lakes, caimans are on the move.

A tale of two seasons

No one knows how many caimans live in the Pantanal, but the figure is probably at least 100 000, perhaps many more. Close relatives of alligators, caimans are smaller, rarely growing more than 2.5 m long. Like alligators, they are adaptable animals that can live in places that are permanently wet, or places – like the Pantanal – that are dry for several months each year. Many caimans spend the Pantanal's dry season in isolated pools, burrowing into the mud if the pool should completely dry out.

Adult caimans mate at the end of the dry season, and the females lay between 20 and 40 eggs each year. They build a nest mound from plants and stand guard over the nest until the eggs have hatched. Instead of fending off other females,

WETLAND PLEASURES There is no shortage of prey for a spectacled caiman in the Pantanal's wet season. In the dry season, shallow lakes shrink under cloudless skies (opposite), stranding caimans and other aquatic creatures.

caimans will share a nest and the mothers join forces to defend it. It is important work as the nutrient-packed eggs attract the interest of many predators, including Tegu lizards, coatis and foxes. By the time the young caimans hatch, the annual flood is subsiding. Watched over by the females, the hatchlings immediately start searching for food. They are only 15 cm long, but already have sharp teeth that can grip freshwater insects and their grubs. Common caimans grow up quickly, reaching adulthood in just four years.

THE PANTANAL

OKAVANGO

THE OKAVANGO DELTA IN NORTHERN BOTSWANA IS ONE OF NATURE'S MOST REMARKABLE GRAND FINALES – a place where an entire river fans out across the landscape and then gradually disappears. The Okavango is not the world's only inland delta, but it is the largest and by far the richest in wildlife, home to all of Africa's 'big five' mammals – lions, leopards, elephants, Cape buffalo and rhino – as well as its largest snakes and the Nile crocodile. In some parts of the delta, antelope seem to be everywhere: the lush swampy grassland is the natural home of the water-loving lechwe, but it attracts antelope from drier habitats as well. They all depend on one thing: water that falls in the highlands of Angola, 800 km away. This water travels south in the Okavango River until it reaches the fringes of the Kalahari Desert. Here, it spreads out like a giant irrigation system – one that works all year.

From space, the delta looks like a bright green hand, contrasting with the Kalahari's yellowish-brown desert sand. The 'hand' is created by dozens of separate channels, which split off from the Okavango before wandering over the table-flat terrain. These tributaries-in-reverse feed countless pools and

AMPHIBIOUS ANTELOPE Startled by a boat, lechwe leap for safety. These antelope often feed up to their haunches in water. They have large hooves that stop them sinking into soft mud.

FOLLOW THE LEADER Cape buffalo need lots of water to help them digest their food. Here, a herd is on the move, with large males – called pathfinders – leading the way.

lagoons; the further they are from the main river channel, the slower they flow. At the same time, they lose water through evaporation and also through the porous sand. Eventually, there comes a point where the water coming in is exactly balanced by the water going out. This is the edge of the delta's standing water, and the place where dry land begins.

That, at least, is the theory. But the Okavango delta is like a living organism, growing and shrinking in a complex yearly cycle linked to the local wet and dry seasons and also to the floodwater arriving from faraway Angola. The northern end of the delta is the earliest to get the floodwater – it starts to expand in April each year. The flooding then spreads through the entire delta, taking up to four months to ripple outwards to its furthest edges. As the water gently rises and pools fill up, millions of water lilies burst into bloom. Antelope and buffalo wade between islands to feed, while beneath the surface crocodiles hunt for prey.

PEAT HAS TWO FACES – ONE LIGHT, DRY AND CRUMBLY, THE OTHER SOAKING WET AND TREACHEROUS UNDERFOOT. The latter is the kind found in peat bogs, spongy landscapes hiding pools that can swallow the unwary, some deep enough to cover a truck.

Peat forms from the remains of wetland plants. When the plants die they start to disintegrate, but because they are waterlogged, bacteria cannot completely break them down. Instead, the plant debris accumulates, slowly turning into peat. It's a slow process, adding a paper-thin layer each year. Peat is stained brown by plant chemicals called tannins, but the surface is often covered by reeds, or by a bright green mantle of moss. This may look solid enough to walk on, but appearances are deceptive – under the slightest pressure, the moss parts and the surface can suddenly give way.

From tundra to tropics

Most of the world's peat bogs are in places with cold, damp climates, where the ground never gets a chance to dry out. This kind of scenery is found all around the Northern Hemisphere, from Scandinavia to Alaska and Siberia. Many bogs date back nearly 12 000 years, to the end of the last ice age. As the glaciers retreated, they left bare rock in their wake until mosses and lichens moved in. The result is a landscape of enormous blanket bogs that stretch from one horizon to another,

MAKING PEAT Bogs are inhabited by specialist plants. Sphagnum moss (inset) is the main peat producer in places with cold, damp climates. This brightly coloured moss can hold up to 20 times its own weight in water.

PEAT BOGS

DELICATE HUNTER An adult large red damselfly clings to a leaf after its final larval moult (the intact shed skin is visible in the lower right of the picture). Like all damselflies, this species spends its early life underwater, before taking to the air in spring.

interspersed with rocky outcrops and dark, peat-stained pools. In bad weather, it looks bleak and forlorn, but on a clear day, peat country has a haunting beauty that comes from the open deserted scenery and the far-carrying calls of birds.

Peat bogs are found in the far south of the globe, on islands in the Southern Ocean, and also in the tropics. In 1909, a German dinosaur-hunting expedition to East Africa photographed a peat bog close to the Equator. Peat bogs are widespread in Indonesia and South America, but instead of moss, these bogs are covered with trees. The wildlife includes parrots, orang-utans and tenacious leeches that suck blood from human skin. It is hard to imagine a bigger contrast with the bogs of Ireland or Canada, but they form for the same reason: because the waterlogged conditions stop dead plants rotting down.

Most peat bogs follow the ground's contours like a soggy blanket, but there is another type in which the peat is shaped like a dome. Many of these raised bogs formed over the sites of ancient lakes, building up slowly after a lake filled with sediment and became overgrown with plants.

Buried evidence

For centuries people have cut and dried peat for fuel. In north-west Europe, traditional peat-cutters work with narrow spades, stacking up bricks of peat in open piles to dry. Occasionally, a peat-cutter's spade will hit something solid, such as wood from ancient trees. Known as bog oak, the wood is dark and hard despite being buried for thousands of years.

Europe's peat-cutters have discovered some truly stunning remains. In 1950, two men cutting peat in northern Denmark found the perfectly preserved body of a man. Thinking that it was a murder victim, they reported it to the police. Tollund Man – as he came to be known – had indeed been murdered, but more than 2300 years ago, perhaps as a ritual sacrifice. The acids in the peat bog stopped his body decomposing.

Giant remains

Peat bogs have yielded far older remains than Tollund Man. Hundreds of Irish elk skeletons have been found in bogs across the Northern Hemisphere. Irish elk – the world's largest-ever deer – became extinct about 10 000 years ago. Males stood about 2 m at the shoulder and had large, heavy antlers, each bigger than a car door. Researchers think that these giant deer probably waded into lakes to feed or to get away from biting insects, and that occasionally one would get stuck and sink into the mud on the bottom. Later, the lakes filled with plants that built up peat layers with the deer locked away inside.

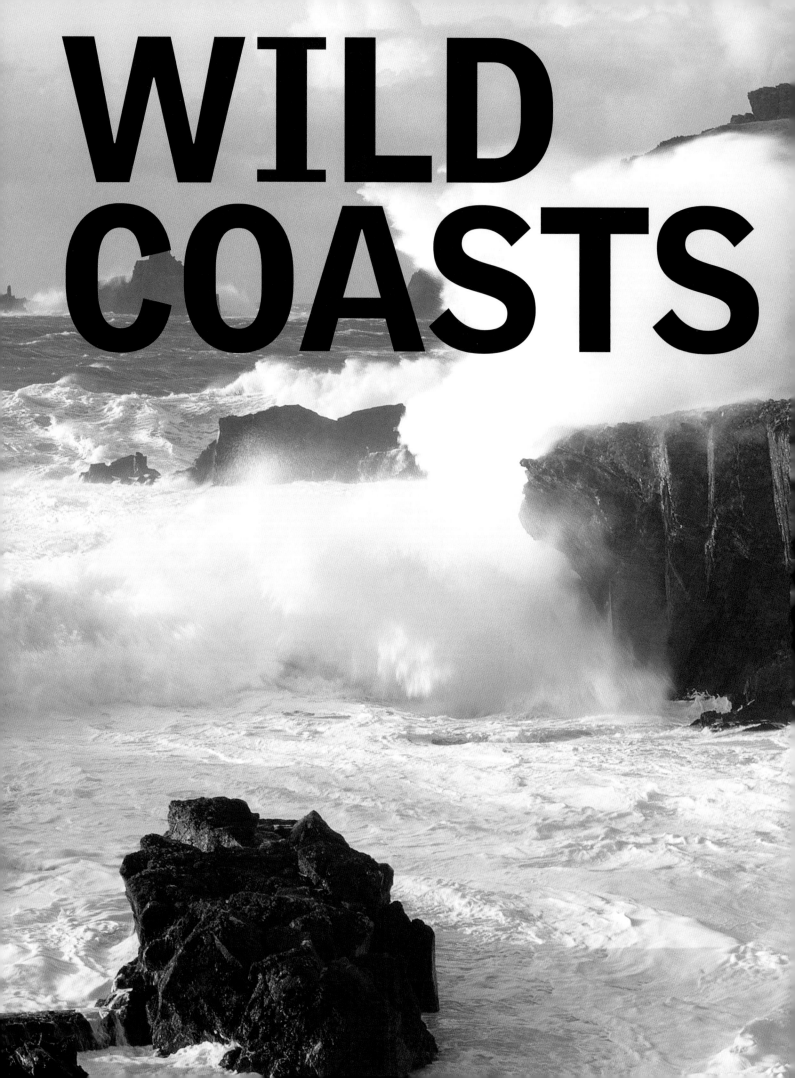

WILD
COASTS

8

MOUNTAINOUS WAVES WHIPPED UP BY WINDS BLOWING ACROSS THE NORTH ATLANTIC POUND IRELAND'S DINGLE PENINSULA (left). Exposed shores like this are wild frontier zones, where the sea eats away at cliffs, smashing rocks apart, undermining some parts of the coast and building up others. The sea can also shape the climate. On temperate coasts like Ireland's, warm currents bring heat from the tropics, while cold polar currents lock other coasts in ice or create sea fog that hangs over desert shores. Ever since people first built boats, the world's coasts have claimed human lives, and some places – such as Cape Horn at South America's southern tip – have earned a fearsome reputation. Modern technology has overcome some of the dangers of these shores, but they are still the ultimate expression of the age-old battle between land and sea.

A COASTAL VIEW MAY LOOK PERMANENT, BUT IT CAN CHANGE IN THE BLINK OF AN EYE WHEN CLIFFS OR ROCK STACKS SUDDENLY GIVE WAY. All around the globe, rocky shores bear the scars of these decisive moments, which are rarely witnessed at first hand because the coastlines are often so remote and rugged. Among the few exceptions are places that attract lots of visitors. In recent times, one of the most unnerving collapses happened on the coast of Victoria, Australia, an area famous for its limestone cliffs, which face the full force of the Southern Ocean. In 1990, two sightseers found themselves stranded on a newly created island, when a natural arch caved in behind them, cutting them off from the rest of the coast. They were lucky: if they had been on the arch, it is unlikely they would have survived. In the event, a helicopter winched them to safety. In 2005, another collapse on this coast destroyed one of the giant rock stacks known as the Twelve Apostles. Only eight of the stacks are still standing, all of them on borrowed time.

WESTERN SHORES Sea stacks and tree-topped rocky islets line the shore in Olympic National Park, Washington State, USA. The power of breakers rolling in from the vast expanses of the Pacific has helped to carve one of North America's most rugged coastlines.

SHIFTING SHORES

BUFFER ZONE Cape Hatteras off North Carolina forms the tip of a slender barrier island between the Atlantic and the US mainland.

In southern England, collapses often happen on the so-called Jurassic Coast, a stretch of the Dorset and East Devon shoreline known for its fossils. A 400 m section of cliff gave way here in May 2008, creating a pile of debris on the beach and attracting fossil-hunters from all over Britain. Farther along the same coast, the scars survive of an even bigger landslip in 1839, which carried away woodland and fields full of ripening corn. Instead of breaking up, the land stayed in one piece, allowing farmers to climb down and harvest their crops, far below the level where they were originally sown.

The power of the sea

Nearly all the world's most rugged stretches of coast have one thing in common: they face the open ocean and the prevailing wind. In places like these, the wind may have travelled over thousands of miles of unbroken water – enough for it to impart an extraordinary power to the waves. When a gale is blowing, breakers smash against the coast, compressing pockets of air into cracks in the rock. When the water falls back, the air expands suddenly like an explosive charge. A similar process may be repeated at each high tide, steadily weakening rock near the waterline until it gives way.

It is not just fixed objects that feel the ocean's force. At high tide, the sea can shift boulders weighing hundreds of tonnes, while anything that floats, such as driftwood, soon has all its sharp edges rolled smooth. In North America's Pacific North-

West, some of the world's tallest conifers grow close to the shore. After storms, trees sometimes topple over and end up on the beach. Every time the tide comes in, the sea rearranges the giant tree trunks as if they were matchsticks, then it leaves them in precariously balanced piles as it retreats down the shore.

Shaped by the sea

In some parts of the world, the sea is eating into entire coastlines. Houses topple into the water and over the centuries entire villages and towns have disappeared. No matter how well coasts are defended, the sea finds its way into weak points and levers them open during storms. As well as nibbling chunks out of the coast, the sea can move it about, creating low-lying sandbanks and slender islands that are constantly on the move.

Cape Hatteras on the coast of North Carolina, USA, has a reputation for being one of the most dangerous of these shifting shores. Jutting out into the Atlantic, it lies at the meeting point of two different currents – the cold Labrador Current, which flows down from the Arctic, and the Gulf Stream, sweeping northwards from the tropics. Over the centuries, hundreds of ships have foundered on its moving sandbanks – sometimes within a stone's throw of the shore. Its lighthouse, built in 1870, came close to being a victim and in 1999 was moved almost 1 km inland to prevent it being claimed by the waves.

In estuaries, the sea works like a brake on the emerging river, pushing against the river water so that it flows backwards and forwards with the tide. When rivers slow in this way, they drop the sediment they are carrying, creating marshy land that spreads outwards from the shore. Estuarine marshes are a magnet for wading birds, which probe for food in the mud. This kind of shoreline can be one of the wildest of all.

NORTHERN REFUGE A satellite image shows the vast delta of Siberia's River Lena where it fans out into the Arctic Ocean. Millions of migratory birds come here to breed.

EVEN IN AN AGE OF GLOBAL WARMING, THOUSANDS OF MILES OF COASTLINE FREEZE UP EVERY YEAR. During the southern winter, ice spreads out from the coast of Antarctica from March onwards. In the north, the annual freeze-up begins in October, eventually reaching as far south as Labrador and the shores of Hudson Bay in Canada, well outside the Arctic Circle.

Labrador is on a similar latitude to Cornwall, England, and it has the same kind of rocky coastline, but there the similarities end. Cornwall is bathed by the Gulf Stream, which originates in the tropical waters of the Gulf of Mexico, lifting the sea's temperature by up to 10°C. The Cornish coast hardly ever experiences frost, and its sheltered valleys are famous for subtropical plants, which need warmth to survive. Some 5000 km to the west, the coast of Labrador is chilled by the Labrador Current, whose icy water originates in the Arctic before flowing down through the gap between Greenland and Baffin Island. In winter, the coast here is locked in a frozen apron, known as 'landfast ice', which grows outwards to meet floating ice, or 'pack ice', which forms at sea.

In most parts of the Arctic and Antarctic, the two kinds of ice join up, but in some places strong coastal currents keep them apart. The result is jagged areas of open water, called 'shore leads', which attract an array of wildlife, from tiny crustaceans to narwhals and other whales. The bigger gaps, called 'polynyas' (the Russian word for 'ice hole'), are like miniature seas, filled with animals that cannot survive in

FROZEN COASTS

ICEBERG NURSERY Ice lies scattered across Neko Harbour on the Antarctic Peninsula. In late summer, the glacier in the background can calve several icebergs a day.

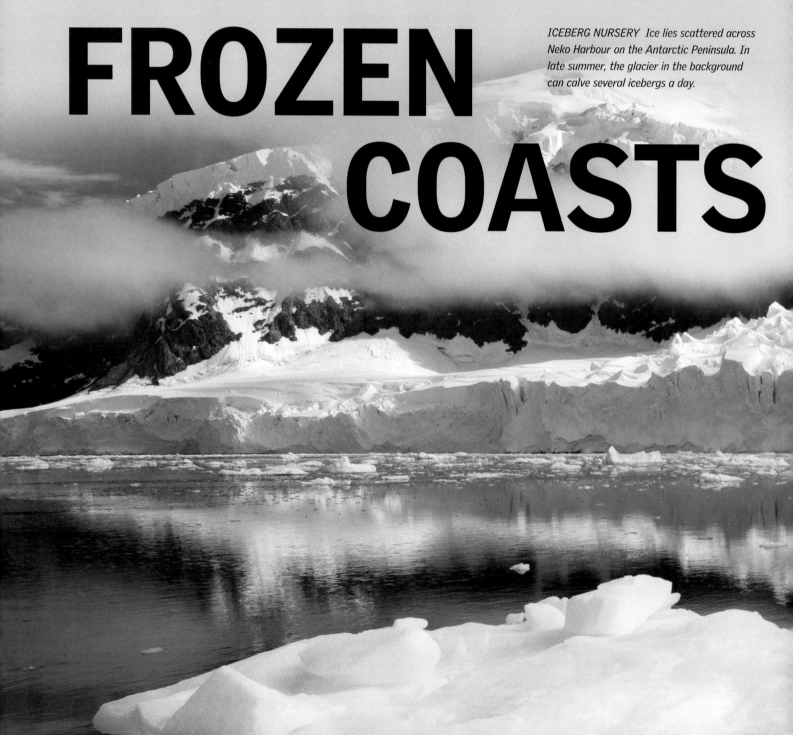

SEA UNICORNS Male narwhals have a single tusk with a built-in spiral twist. Up to 3 m long, the tusk is probably used to impress and see off rival males.

places where the water freezes over. The largest, the North Water Polynya, forms each winter between Ellesmere Island and Devon Island in Canada and the coast of Greenland, covering about 50 000 km².

Flotillas of icebergs

At both ends of the Earth, the lengthening days of spring signal the start of the iceberg season. Every year, roughly 30 000 icebergs break loose – or are 'calved' – from Greenland's glaciers. Although these can be huge, dwarfing the world's largest ships, they are tiny compared with the flat-topped ice islands that drift away from Antarctica, some of which are more than 200 km long – bigger than many island nations. Icebergs this large can survive for more than 30 years before they finally disintegrate and disappear.

Off Labrador, most icebergs come from glaciers on Greenland's western coast. The Labrador Current picks them up and carries them out into the North Atlantic at an average speed of about 10 km/h. Labrador is thinly populated, but the scattered fishing ports along its eastern shore all look out on the same incredible spectacle of icebergs floating past, like fleets of majestic ships on a one-way journey to the warmer waters of the south. In the past, sailors nicknamed this stretch of North America's coastline Iceberg Alley, and the name has stuck. Today, it is recognised as one of the best places to view icebergs in the Northern Hemisphere.

POUNDED BY ATLANTIC BREAKERS AND SWEPT BY DANGEROUS CURRENTS, Namibia's Skeleton Coast has claimed countless ships in the past 500 years. This wild stretch of African shore fringes the northern part of the Namib Desert. It has one of the world's most arid climates, tempered by dense fogs that roll in from the sea during the night. These fogs are the coast's lifeline, delivering just enough moisture to keep plants and animals alive, but they also make the shoreline treacherous for ships.

The fog is produced when warm air blows off the land just after sunset and meets the cold, northward-flowing waters of the Benguela Current – part of a huge circle, or gyre, which circulates in an anti-clockwise direction around the South Atlantic. The effect is almost instantaneous: the air chills rapidly, just like breath on a winter's day. This creates large banks of moisture, which by dawn are being blown back inland, wrapping the entire coast in clouds of fog that take several hours to burn away.

Waters to avoid

There are no records of the first boats to sail down the Skeleton Coast. The region's original inhabitants bred cattle and goats and, unlike many other coastal peoples in Africa, had no tradition of seafaring. The first Europeans to arrive were Portuguese navigators, who found one of the few safe anchorages – a rocky

SKELETON COAST

HAZARDOUS SHORE Namibia's Skeleton Coast may have plenty of sun, sand and surf, but its vast, empty beaches attract few visitors. One victim of this dangerous coastline was the Dunedin Star, *which ran aground in 1942, carrying wartime munitions and evacuees from the Blitz. All of the crew and passengers eventually made it to safety.*

COASTAL SURVIVORS An old wreck makes a handy perch for cormorants. Scavenging jackels (below) feed on the remains of a fur seal.

point called Cape Cross in modern-day Namibia – in 1486. Since then, most sailors have tried to avoid the Skeleton Coast, with its dangerous fogs and arid dunes. Vessels that ventured too close have often come to grief, and the shore is lined with wrecks – now used by Cape cormorants and other seabirds as nesting sites. But it is real skeletons, as well as those of ships, that gave the coast its name. As the Benguela Current flows along the Skeleton Coast, it brings cold deep water towards the surface, and with this water come dissolved nutrients that nourish huge quantities of plankton and immense numbers of fish. Portuguese seafarers noticed this, and they also saw that the offshore waters teemed with fur seals and whales. The coast's macabre name comes from their washed-up skeletons.

As in many other parts of the world, the discovery of fur seals and whales along the Skeleton Coast was the prelude to

reckless exploitation (see page 23). The fur seals were particularly easy to hunt, because they gathered in vast breeding colonies, hemmed in by the Namib Desert or on islands farther south. Their numbers plunged dramatically, until declining demand for their fur and oil allowed them to stage a comeback. Nowadays, at the height of the breeding season, the largest breeding colony, at Cape Cross, has up to 200 000 Cape fur seals – reputed to be one of the biggest and smelliest collections of sea mammals in the world.

Compared with this incredible abundance on the beaches and in the offshore waters, life inland is thinly spread. Two of the region's land mammals – the black-backed jackal and brown hyena – patrol the shore for dead remains and thus live indirectly on food from the sea. Farther inland, among the desert's sand dunes and gravel plains, the influence of the sea fades. Here, life is based on desert plants and lichens that animals can feed on. Since lichens do not have roots, they cannot reach deep down to get at water. Instead, as the fog rolls inland each dawn, they open up to absorb as much moisture as they can. In the hours just after daylight, the gravel plains often have a greenish-grey tinge until the lichens curl up and their colour seems to fade away.

ROCKS AND REEFS

TENACIOUS GRIP Mussels, starfish and giant sea anemones cling to a submerged rock off the coast of Oregon, USA. The starfish are differently coloured varieties of the same species.

RUINOUSLY SHARP Fang-like rocks, such as these off Orkney, are found where the layers in the rock are tilted at an angle to the sea. They can easily tear through the hull of a wooden ship.

HIDDEN BENEATH THE SWEEP OF SHIPBORNE RADARS, offshore rocks and reefs present some of the worst hazards when sailing close to coasts. But what is a lurking threat to shipping offers a home to a range of wildlife, from barnacles and mussels to cormorants and giant turtles.

During the age of sail, rocks were immense navigational dangers, because ships dependent on the power of the wind could easily be driven onto them by the wind and tides. The lighthouse was invented to reduce this risk; it existed in ancient times, but almost always on the shore. Then, in the late 17th century, seafaring European nations began to build lighthouses on the rocks themselves. The earliest did not last long. In British waters, the first wooden lighthouse built on the notorious Eddystone Rocks off south-eastern Cornwall survived just five years – a huge storm swept it away in 1703. Three further lighthouses followed on the Eddystone Rocks, each with a stronger design than the one before. The fourth dates from 1882 and is still in use.

Barnacle cement

Like all its modern counterparts, the Eddystone Lighthouse is fixed in place with cement, a substance that can harden underwater to produce an almost unbreakable bond. Rock-dwelling animals, such as acorn barnacles (*Semibalanus balanoides*), have been using something similar for hundreds of millions of years.

Unlike animals of the open water, those that fasten themselves to rocks are fully exposed to the power of the waves, which during the most violent winter storms can strike the rocks with a force equivalent to a fast-moving motor car. It takes exceptional strength to ride out conditions like these, but acorn barnacles succeed in holding on in places where all other creatures would be dislodged. These small volcano-shaped relatives of crabs and lobsters, each individual protected by a case of chalky plates, can be amazingly numerous. On some rocks, more than 5000 barnacles are crammed into every square metre, taking up almost all the room. Their extraordinary strength comes from a chemical cement, made by their young, or larvae. These drift in the sea until they meet a rock where, if it is suitable, they fasten themselves in place. The larva makes its cement in glands in its head and once the cement has set, the barnacle begins to build its chalky plates. From this moment onwards, it is fixed to the rock for the rest of its life.

Barnacles feed by collecting particles drifting in the water – a way of life that allows them to stay in the same place.

Mussels also live like this, but they attach themselves using a mass of tough but flexible threads, called a beard or byssus – from the Greek *bussos*, meaning 'flax'. The threads anchor the mussel to the rock like the guy ropes of a tent. Although the byssus is superb at withstanding the tug of the waves, mussels do occasionally get detached, in which case they simply make more threads and set up home elsewhere.

Most other rock-dwellers – including limpets, sea anemones and starfish – creep over rocks in a slow-motion ballet, actively searching for their food. Instead of being cemented to the rock, they use adjustable suckers. Starfish have some of the smallest suckers at the tips of fluid-filled 'tube feet'. Individually, these are quite weak, but because a starfish has several hundred of them its overall grip is extremely strong. At the other extreme, some of the biggest suckers belong to two kinds of mollusc – chitons and abalones. When fully grown, they can have suckers as large as a man's hand. Chitons are so tough that very few people would eat them from choice, but abalones have been collected for food since prehistoric times.

Life on the rocks

Apart from seals, few mammals live on coastal rocks and only one reptile – the marine iguana of the Galápagos Islands. Birds, by contrast, abound. Herons and gulls feed in rock pools, while oystercatchers use their brightly coloured beaks to smash open mussels at low tide. All over the world, offshore rocks also attract various species of cormorant, sometimes in huge numbers.

Cormorants use rocks as platforms from which to dive into the waves for fish and – just as importantly – as places to perch and dry off when they come out of the water. They feed underwater, using their webbed feet to propel them to depths of as much as 30 m as they chase individual fish. Unlike most diving birds, they have feathers that are only partly waterproof. When a cormorant dives, the feathers become sleek and streamlined, but they stay wet when it clambers back onto a rock. To get around this problem, cormorants hold their wings open to help them to dry. They often do this just beyond the reach of the waves, where they look like dark statues, waiting for a signal to move.

Cormorants include some of the world's most widespread coastal birds, as well as some species that are restricted to tiny specks of land in the oceans. One of these, the Bounty Island shag (*Phalacrocorax ranfurlyi*), is found only on the Bounty Islands – a small group of islets and rocks south-west of New Zealand, discovered by Captain William Bligh just before the mutiny on board his ship. Another species, the flightless

Each coral polyp protects itself by building a hard chalky cup. In a reef, these cups accumulate over the centuries, creating the most massive structures made by living things.

cormorant (*Phalacrocorax harrisi*), lives only in the Galápagos Islands. It has tiny wings and, as its name suggests, cannot fly.

Below the waterline

Unlike rocks, coral reefs are level with the sea's surface, only rising above it at low tide – at high tide, the warning sign of their presence is breaking surf. Reefs are built by small animals called polyps, which need warmth and sunshine to survive.

Individually, coral polyps are quite fragile, but each one protects itself by building a hard chalky cup. In a reef, these cups accumulate over the centuries, creating the most massive structures made by living things. At 2000 km long, Australia's Great Barrier Reef is by far the largest and most famous, but even much smaller reefs have mind-boggling dimensions. If reefs could be lifted out of the sea and weighed on land, many would weigh millions of tonnes.

Although a vast number of fish and other animals live in the crevices and caves of a reef, only the outer 'skin' in a healthy reef is actually alive – this is where the polyps are still active. The graceful appearance of coral conceals a hard edge, often sharp enough to rip open human skin or even smash through wooden hulls. One of the world's greatest navigators, Captain James Cook, experienced this when he and his shipmates became the first Europeans to set eyes on the Great Barrier Reef in 1770. While their ship, the *Endeavour*, was picking its way through the reef's winding channels, it hit the coral and became stuck fast. The crew was able to refloat the ship, but after limping back to the mainland, a large piece of coral was discovered still plugging the hole in the hull.

Corals in the air

Occasionally, geological movements lift the seabed, leaving coral high and dry. Perched above water level, coral quickly dies and its remains become a platform of sun-bleached rock. Essentially the same material as limestone, the coral is dissolved by rain over the centuries, creating jagged crevices that nurture tropical plants.

Aldabra Atoll in the Indian Ocean is the largest of these reefs perched above the sea. The atoll

CORAL MAZE Channels cut through Australia's Great Barrier Reef like deep blue rivers. Tidal currents flow along them, circulating water through the reef.

THIRSTY ISLAND Aldabra's raised coral islets are porous, so hold almost no freshwater. Any plants that live here have to catch their own water when it rains.

(see pages 28–29) consists of four slender islands, arranged in the shape of a flattened horseshoe. Inside them is a lagoon more than 30 km across, peppered with dozens of coral islets whose names date from French colonial times. Some, like Île aux Cèdres ('Cedar Island') and Île Verte ('Green Island'), sound enticing, but one – Champignon des Os ('Mushroom of Bones') – gives a hint that Aldabra is not as welcoming as it might seem.

At close range, many of the islets look as if they have been specifically designed to repel human boarders. Over the millennia, the sea has eaten into the coral between the high and low tidemarks, creating mushroom-like platforms topped with jagged coral and twisted leathery-leaved plants. This is not travel-brochure territory. There are no people, apart from the occasional scientist, and certainly no hotels, but Aldabra has something special – an extraordinary collection of its own plants and animals, including the largest group of giant tortoises left in the world.

Several centuries ago, giant tortoises lived on several groups of islands scattered throughout the tropical seas. Unfortunately, these huge reptiles were

prized as fresh meat by sailors and they were plundered whenever their homes were discovered. In the 16th century, when Spanish navigators found the Galápagos, the islands were home to about 250 000 giant tortoises. Today, only about 15 000 are left. Things were even worse in the Indian Ocean. Wild tortoises once lived in the Seychelles, Mauritius, Rodrigues and Réunion, but now they are either extinct or survive only in captivity. Protected by the fortress-like structures of Aldabra's coral islands, the giant tortoises there managed to avoid this fate. There are at least 100 000 of them, and they live on all four of the main islands. Males weigh up to quarter of a tonne and can live to a ripe age of 100, foraging on the islands' plants.

MAN-MADE REEFS Sunken ships soon become encrusted with sponges and corals. Here, a diver in the Red Sea inspects the wreck of the Umbria, an Italian ship scuttled during World War II.

CAPE HORN

CAPE HORN HOLDS A SPECIAL PLACE IN SEAFARING LEGEND. **The southernmost major cape in the South American landmass,** it is the world's only major cape outside Antarctica where there is nothing to the east or west of it but sea circling the whole globe. Unimpeded by any contact with land, endless storms blow in on the westerly wind, battering the cape and making the surrounding stretch of coastline one of the most dangerous places for shipping on Earth.

Before the opening of the Panama Canal in 1914, 'rounding the Horn' was a rite of passage on board ships sailing between the Atlantic and the Pacific. Its golden age as a shipping route was in the mid-19th century, when clippers – the world's fastest sailing ships – operated between Europe

and North America's eastern seaboard and the Far East, carrying tea from Asia and wool from Australia. They used a route that took them far into the Southern Ocean, where they were able to exploit its ferocious winds. With the wind behind it, a clipper leaving Australia could reach Cape Horn in just 20 days, before entering the Atlantic and heading north.

Another boost to the sea route round Cape Horn came in 1849 when gold was discovered in California. Thousands of would-be prospectors chose to go around the bottom of South America, rather than making the long and difficult overland journey across North America. But this boom was short-lived.

DANGER ZONE Cape Horn is infamous for giant waves that, through the combined effects of ocean currents and wind, pile up without warning.

he gold rush subsided, and railroads made it safer and faster to ravel by land. When the Panama Canal opened, the Cape Horn oute finally became obsolete. Today, rounding the Horn is an chievement prized by adventurous yachtsmen and women.

sland jigsaw

Although part of the South American landmass, Cape Horn is not ctually attached to the mainland. Instead of coming to a neat onclusion, the tip of South America disintegrates into a jigsaw f rocky islands and channels – scenery that is typical of oastlines gouged out by glacial ice. During the last ice age, the vhole of this region was covered by the Patagonian Ice Sheet, vhich extended northwards over the Andes. When the ice ventually started to melt, the sea invaded the deepest coastal alleys, creating the islands that exist today.

In the far south, the biggest island is Tierra del Fuego, hared by Chile and Argentina. One of the first scientists to xplore the interior of Tierra del Fuego was the English biologist Charles Darwin in 1832 during his round-the-world voyage on the Royal Navy's survey ship, HMS *Beagle*. He was struck not only by he island's grandeur, but also by its harsh climate. It can snow ven in mid-summer, and the maximum temperature at sea level ften struggles to get above 10°C. Because Tierra del Fuego is so ar south, summer days are 18 hours long, but in winter there are ust six hours of daylight and thick cloud often means that the Gun hardly seems to shine at all. In these chilly onditions, small remnants of the Patagonian Ice Sheet still linger on the island's peaks. The highest, Mount Darwin, is surrounded by ice, which creeps lowly downhill towards the shore.

When the clouds part, Mount Darwin gives superb view of the Beagle Channel – named after Darwin's ship, whose primary mission was to survey nd chart the waters off South America. On the far side of the channel lies a cluster of rocky outcrops, alled the Wollaston Islands. Here, amid mountainous vaves, is Isla Hornos or Cape Horn Island.

Feasts of kelp

Despite its punishing climate, the tip of South America teems with life, particularly in the sea. Close to the waterline, giant seaweeds swirl to and fro in the current. These seaweeds, known as kelps, are specially adapted for life on exposed rocky coasts. Their fronds are amazingly strong, and they anchor themselves with rubbery structures, called holdfasts, which grip submerged boulders or rocks like many-fingered hands. They do not have seeds – instead, kelps develop from tiny spores released into the water.

When kelps are still very young, they are small enough to be 'grazed' by sea urchins and other animals that creep over the surface of the rocks, while groups of kelp geese peck at them with short hook-tipped beaks. These stocky birds are distant relatives of the common shelduck found in Europe and are the same shape and size – somewhere between a duck and a domestic goose. Male kelp geese are completely white, but the females are dark brown, which helps them to hide from predators when they are sitting on their eggs.

Unimpeded by any contact with land, endless storms batter Cape Horn, making the surrounding stretch of coastline one of the most dangerous places for shipping on Earth.

their southernmost piece of land, Islote Águila (Eagle Islet), is also the southernmost point in South America.

The final crossing

What lay beyond South America at the world's southernmost extreme? Until the 16th century, many European map-makers assumed that there must be an unknown landmass to balance the land in the Northern Hemisphere. The discovery of Cape Horn seemed to disprove this, because there appeared to be no land at all beyond the cape and the Diego Ramírez Islands. In the late 18th century, seal-hunters showed that this was wrong when they discovered a host of new islands much farther south. Then, in 1820, the crews of three ships (one Russian, one British and one American) on three separate expeditions all set eyes on a new continent: Antarctica. The Russian expedition, led by Fabian Gottlieb von Bellingshausen, was the first to do so, on January 27.

Although Antarctica is nearly 1000 km from Cape Horn, some animal travellers regularly make the journey between South America and the icy south. One is the giant petrel, an aggressive predator, which often eats penguin chicks as well as the dead remains of whales and seals. Another is the snowy sheathbill, a snow-white scavenger shaped rather like a chicken, which spends the winter in South America, returning to Antarctica in summer to breed. The only Antarctic bird without webbed feet, the sheathbill cannot swim and feeds entirely on land – often by harassing penguins so that they cough up their catch. Its twice-yearly flight between South America and Antarctica is a major endurance test as it crosses the world's stormiest stretch of sea in the teeth of violent westerly winds. Unlike albatrosses, which soar over the ocean with spectacular ease, a sheathbill has to flap hard until it reaches its journey's end.

The halfway point of this crossing is marked by a boundary that has no equivalent in the Northern Hemisphere. Called the Antarctic Convergence, it marks the point where cold Antarctic currents reach their farthest north, before sinking down into the ocean's depths. The convergence is between 30 km and 50 km wide, and the temperature difference in the water on either side of it can be as much as 5°C. As well as being important for marine wildlife, this oceanic frontier can also be seen as a threshold in human history. To the north is Tierra del Fuego, the southernmost point on Earth that humans managed to reach on foot before the great age of exploration. To the south is Antarctica, the greatest wilderness on Earth, never even sighted by humans until 1820.

Kelp geese are good fliers, but another visitor to the kelp beds, the flightless steamerduck, is unable to get into the air. It feeds by diving and spends most of its time offshore.

To the ends of the Earth

When Darwin visited Tierra del Fuego, the island was still populated by native Yaghan Indians, who had fished its shores for millennia using bark canoes. The Yaghans became famous for their tolerance of cold, diving for shellfish in temperatures that would give most people thermal shock. But hardiness in the face of the elements could not protect them from European diseases. When settlers from the north arrived on Tierra del Fuego, the Yaghans' numbers declined rapidly and today there are no full-blooded survivors left.

It is not known when Europeans first reached the waters around Cape Horn. In 1520, a Spanish expedition sailed through the channel that separates northern Tierra del Fuego from the Chilean mainland during the first circumnavigation of the globe – the 570 km channel was named the Strait of Magellan after the expedition's Portuguese commander, Ferdinand Magellan. The first Europeans to sight Cape Horn itself may have been the crew of a Spanish ship, the *San Lesmes*, which was blown off course during a storm five years later. They reported seeing a rocky headland at 56 degrees south – the latitude of Cape Horn. South of this, they saw nothing but open sea. In 1578, the English seafarer, Sir Francis Drake, during his circumnavigation of the globe, also concluded that there was no land south of Cape Horn.

As it turned out, both Drake and the crew of the *San Lesmes* were wrong – but only just. In 1619, a Spanish expedition discovered a bleak cluster of cloud-covered rocks about 100 km south-west of the cape. Now known as the Diego Ramírez Islands (after the expedition's cosmographer), they lie on South America's continental shelf. This means that in geological terms

FLIGHTLESS
STEAMERDUCK

LIVING ONLY IN THE EXTREME SOUTH

OF SOUTH AMERICA AND IN THE FALKLAND ISLANDS, THE STEAMERDUCKS ARE A SMALL AND VERY UNUSUAL GROUP. There are four species altogether. One can fly, although it does its best to avoid it, and the other three – the flightless steamerduck, the Falkland steamerduck and the Chubut steamerduck – never take to the air. Weighing up to 7 kg, flightless steamerducks are bigger than many geese, with powerfully built bodies and bright yellow legs but small wings. If one is threatened, it escapes across the water by paddling furiously with its legs and 'rowing' with its wings. Its noisy splashing creates a wake like an old-fashioned paddle steamer, which is how these ducks earned their name.

Steamerducks feed in the same way as the eiders of the Northern Hemisphere, by diving down to the seabed, where they collect shellfish and other animals. Their beaks are strong enough to crush a finger, and they make short work of molluscs and crabs. They often feed in kelp beds, loafing on rocks when the tide is in and feeding when it falls. The flying steamerducks head inland during the breeding season to nest by freshwater lakes, but the flightless species all lay their eggs close to the sea. During the breeding season, male steamerducks can be highly aggressive and often fight each other on the water. They have a large bony knob on the bend of each wing, which they use as weapons, sometimes battering each other so hard that they draw blood.

CLASS: Aves
ORDER: Anserisformes
SPECIES: *Tachyeres brachypterus*
HABITAT: Rocky coasts with sheltered inlets and kelp beds
DISTRIBUTION: Southern Chile, Beagle Channel and waters around Tierra del Fuego
KEY FEATURE: Sturdy coastal duck that has lost the ability to fly

INDEX

PICTURE CREDITS

NATURE'S MIGHTY POWERS: EARTH'S WILD PLACES
was published by The Reader's Digest Association Ltd, London. It was created and produced for Reader's Digest by Toucan Books Ltd, London.

The Reader's Digest Association Ltd,
11 Westferry Circus,
Canary Wharf,
London E14 4HE
www.readersdigest.co.uk

Copyright © 2009 The Reader's Digest Association Ltd

Written by
David Burnie

FOR TOUCAN BOOKS
Editors Jane Chapman, Celia Coyne, Helen Douglas-Cooper, Andrew Kerr-Jarrett
Designers Bradbury & Williams
Picture researchers Angela Anderson, Wendy Palmer, Sharon Southren, Mia Stewart-Wilson, Christine Vincent
Proofreader Marion Dent
Indexer Michael Dent

FOR READER'S DIGEST
Project editor Christine Noble
Art editor Julie Bennett
Pre-press account manager Dean Russell
Product production manager Claudette Bramble
Production controller Katherine Bunn

READER'S DIGEST, GENERAL BOOKS
Editorial director Julian Browne
Art director Anne-Marie Bulat

Colour origination Colour Systems Ltd, London
Printed and bound in China

We are committed to both the quality of our products and the service we provide to our customers. We value your comments, so please feel free to contact us on 08705 113366 or via our website at **www.readersdigest.co.uk**

If you have any comments or suggestions about the content of our books, you can email us at **gbeditorial@readersdigest.co.uk**

CONCEPT CODE: UK0138/G/S
BOOK CODE: 636-013 UP0000-1
ISBN: 978-0-276-44330-5
ORACLE CODE: 356500006H.00.24